SKEGNESS
THROUGH THE YEARS

Two volumes about the early history of Skegness

Skegness U3A Local History Group

Contents

Introduction

Skegness University of the Third Age (U3A) Local History Group produced a number of documents during the period 2005 to 2008. These included: *Notes on the Local History of Skegness from the earliest times to 1939* (2005) and *Skegness through the Years* (2007).

The first document seeks to bring together the main threads of what was known, mainly from published sources, about the development of Skegness up to 1939.

Skegness through the Years contains more in-depth studies of Skegness in the seventeenth and eighteenth centuries; the transition from agricultural village to a seaside town and short articles on men of influence: the Earls of Scarbrough, Henry Vivian Tippet and Rowland Henry Jenkins.

The Local History Group was dormant between 2010 and 2015. A new group was set up towards the end of 2015 under the leadership of Paul Marshall. As stocks of the documents produced by the earlier group have been exhausted, we have decided to publish the two main documents together in this one volume, so that they can continue to be available to the new group and anyone else interested in the history of Skegness.

In the interest of consistency, some of the figures in the first document have been updated to take account of subsequent work in the later document.

I would like to thank Jon Mackley for his work in bringing this book to publication.

James Mackley

Skegness, October 2016

Volume 1

Notes on the
Local History of Skegness

From the earliest times
to 1939

Skegness U3A Local History
Group

Table of Contents

Foreword

The Skegness Branch of the University of the Third Age (U3A) formed a local history group in 2003. During the period up to the end of 2004, members of the group prepared personal notes, mainly from secondary or tertiary sources, on the history of Skegness. The group decided to draw these notes together in the present document, in the hope that they may be of some interest to readers wanting an introduction to the history of the town. In drawing up this document we have drawn heavily on the work of Winston Kime, whose books provide an authoritative history of Skegness. We are particularly grateful to Mr. Kime for looking through our notes and providing additional comments and corrections. Similarly, we have drawn heavily on Ruth Neller's *Skegness Chronology 1526-1991*, which is available in Skegness Library. We are grateful to Ms Neller for coming to talk to us in February 2005 and for giving us guidance on our future work. Finally, we would like to thank the staff of Skegness Library for their patience in showing us what information is available and giving us access to it.

Skegness, April 2005

Part 1: Skegness and District up to 1653

Early Times

For at least a thousand years up to 500 AD the Lincolnshire coastline extended much farther than it does now. It was fringed by protective sand banks with a shallow lagoon between them and the shore. It is believed that this sheltered shore remained in that state until the late 13th century. The continued sinking and erosive wave action brought the sand back below sea level, so that the waves swept in and battered the shore. So began the long struggle, which culminated in the great flood of 1953.[1]

The ancient inhabitants of Lincolnshire were the *Coritanti* or *Coriceni* and first known about 300 years BC.[2]

Iron Age pottery from Ingoldmells and Skegness has been found. Its association is with salt making by the evaporation of brine. In Roman times, salt producing sites were under direct imperial control.

The Romans invaded England in 55 BC and stayed until AD 435. The Romans encouraged agriculture among local peoples.[3] It is known that the Romans occupied the land near Skegness, as numerous relics have been found.[4]

While the Romans built many banks to stop sea ingress, the

---

[1] Winston Kime: *Skeggy*, Seashell Books, 1969, L. SKEG 9. Winston Kime was born in Skegness, and, apart from Army Service in the last war and several years in Grantham following his retirement, he has lived in the town all his life. His forebears inhabited the Skegness-Wainfleet area for many generations and the parish registers of Skegness show Kimes, or Kymes, going back to the seventeenth century. His whole working career was in the employ of the Skegness Urban District Council, for many years under Rowland Jenkins, town engineer and surveyor, who designed the modern Skegness foreshore, and Winston Kime was actively associated with municipal developments from the late 1920s until his retirement in 1972. A keen cyclist in his younger days, he was a founder member of the local Wheelers in 1933 and is a life vice president of the County Cycling Association. In recent years he has spent much time researching the records of this area. Winston Kime is a widower, with a married daughter, Patricia, and a son, David.
[2] Geo. H. J. Dutton: *Ancient and Modern Skegness and District*, 1916.
[3] *Ibid.*
[4] Information taken from a pamphlet called *The Pier*, designed to promote Skegness and the surrounding countryside: L.SKEG.79.

"Roman Bank" cannot be claimed to have been made by the Romans.[5] However, Burgh, about four and a half miles from Skegness to the west of this road was undoubtedly a Roman military station. The Rev. Tatham suggested that the Roman road from Lincoln to the coast, traceable as far as Orby Lane, just west of Burgh, led to a fort and ferry at Skegness, but its route from that point is a matter for conjecture.[6]

The difficulties in tracing the early history were mostly produced by natural causes:

> The continual encroachment of the sea, which repeatedly altered the coastline and engulfed some towns;
> The drainage of the Fens, which turned miles of barren land into rich fertile plains.

During the Roman occupancy, an elevated road made it possible to reclaim portions of the marshy land. With the withdrawal of the Romans these roads were left to fall into disuse and the land reverted to its original state, so to lie for many centuries.[7]

From Saxons to Roundheads

Saxons and Danes

The Anglo-Saxons invaded England in the fifth century and the kings of Mercia eventually ruled the Skegness area. The Danes, or Northmen, first attacked England in 787. In the ninth and tenth centuries Vikings and Danes invaded on to the sandy shore between Theddlethorpe and Skegness. The Danish presence is seen by the names of towns and villages. The Anglo-Saxons and Danes ruled England up to 1066.[8]

---

[5] Dutton: op. cit.
[6] Comment by Mr Kime in a personal note given to the Chair of the Skegness Branch of the U3A, January 2005.
[7] *The Pier*, op. cit.; Dutton: op. cit.
[8] Dutton: op. cit.

Derivation of Skegness

In the Domesday Book in 1086, during William the Conqueror's reign, Skegness was known as Tric. No mention of Tric has been found before or since 1086.[9]

The name "Skegness" is of Scandinavian origin. The first part of the name could derive from "skeggi" – a beard – though it could also derive from a similar source to "Skaggenak". The second part almost certainly is derived from "ness" – a nose or promontory. In the Middle Ages, the town of Skegness is believed to have been a flourishing and populous port, having a roadstead protected by jutting headlands. It is one of these "nesses" that gave the town the second part of its name.[10]

The word "ness" is used generally, though not exclusively, as a suffix wherever the Norsemen made their way. As might be expected, the counties, which claim the greatest number of "nesses", are Yorkshire and Lincolnshire. Thus, in the county of Lincolnshire, we have Trentness, Durtness, Chowderness, Bellness, Cleeness, Skitterness and Skegness. Occasionally we find the original ness distorted into house or nest; Gunness is often written as Gunhouse, Sandness has been turned into Sandsness, just as Skegness is, sometimes, referred to as Skegsnest.

1066 to 1653

The first written record of Skegness is in a charter granted by Richard I in the tenth year of his reign (1199) to the Abbey of Revesby, by which he confirmed to them their possessions in Skegness. In the reign of Henry III (1216–1272) quite a number of distinguished persons held land in Skegness and in 1316 we read that "John de Orreby possessed at his death 80 acres of pasture land in Skegness. The following year Sir Robert de Wylughby and Margaret his wife was seized of 40 acres of land as one of the co-heirs of John de Orreby". Roger de Somerville, son of Edmund, died seized of the

---

[9] Winston Kime: op. cit.
[10] Dutton: op. cit.; William White: *History, Gazetteer and Directory of Lincolnshire*, 1856.

other moiety in 1338, as did his brother Philip in 1355.[11]

The Courts of the Lord of the Manor of Ingoldmells were frequently held in Skegness. These date back to 1291 and continued for several hundred years.[12]

Skegness in 1430 possessed a port or harbour because Robert Brightsance and William Coke were charged with damaging the harbour but there is nothing to show where. It was possibly situated near Gibraltar Point.[13] Kime suggests that it was situated three or four miles out to sea at the northern tip of what is now known as the Knock Sands.[14]

There is a tradition that Skegness was once a place of importance, with a castle: there is a reference by the chronicler John Leland to the existence of a castle in Skegness.[15] Investigations by the Rev. E.H.R. Tatham seem to confirm the idea that a castle or castellan existed here in the Middle Ages.[16] Most of Skegness came under the jurisdiction of Ingoldmells manor. The court rolls of 1345 mention two different transactions at the same court, concerning land at Chesterland and Castleland. These are thought to refer to land in the area of a castle at Skegness. Tatham also reported another case in 1422 in which William Scalflete surrendered four acres of land at Chesterland. As it was not mentioned by 1422 it is assumed that by then it had succumbed to the sea.[17]

A marginal note in the diocesan records relating to a subsidy collection in 1526 states: "This church and a great part of the parish

---

[11] Abel Heywood and Sons: *Guide to Skegness and Wainfleet* (Series of Illustrated Guidebooks).

[12] Information taken from copies of Newspaper Cuttings in the *Scrapbook* of Mr. G.H.J. Dutton. The copies of the *Scrapbooks* were on display in the Church Farm Museum at Skegness in the summer of 2004.

[13] Ibid.

[14] Winston Kime: *Skeggy*; Mr. Kime has commented that this is by no means certain [pers. comm.].

[15] Mr. Kime has commented "I doubt if there was a castle in the traditional sense and think it more likely that it was the remains of a fort built by the Romans" [pers. comm.].

[16] G.H.J. Dutton: *Scrapbooks*, op. cit.

[17] Winston Kime: *Skeggy*, quoting from *Memorials of Old Lincolnshire*, an article by H.E.R. Tatham (1910).

was submerged in the past year and so it remains".[18] The flood finally destroyed old Skegness in 1536.[19] St. Clement's church was built, partly with stones reclaimed from the old church, on its present site, about half a mile inland from the village.

In 1541, Leland wrote in his *Chronicle*:

Skegness was at sumtyme a great haven toune. Mr. Paynelle sayid onto me that he could prove that there was ons an haven and a toune waullid, also a castelle. The old toune is clene consumid and eten up with the se. Part of a chirch of it stode a late, for old Skegnesse is now buildid a pore new thing. At low water appere yet manifest tokens of olde buildinges.[20]

In the sixteenth century the following, amongst others, had estates in Skegness: John Newdigate Esq., William Smyth DLL, Archdeacon of Lincoln, Michael Arongebyn Esq., Lionel Quadring, Thomas Lyttlebury Esq. and Charles, Duke of Suffolk.[21]

At the time of Elizabeth I (1558-1603), there were 14 families in Skegness. Familiar names included:

John de Orreby
Robert de Wylughby
Lionel Quadring
Nicholas Saunderson (Viscount Castleton).[22]

The Civil War had hardly begun when a Royalist sloop sailed into a creek at Skegness. Boston was a Parliamentary stronghold and from thence a troop of the local militia hurried to Skegness and seized the prize. Sir William Ballingdon and ten Cavaliers, with arms and stores, were quickly hustled off to Boston.[23]

---

[18] Winston Kime: *The Book of Skegness*, Barracuda Books Ltd., 1986, p. 84. (*Ista ecclesia et magna pars parochie fuit demersa anno elapso et sic adhuc remanet.*)

[19] Ruth Neller: *Skegness Chronology 1526 – 1991*; Skegness Library, Ruth Neller, Community Librarian, Mablethorpe.

[20] Quoted by Winston Kime in *Skeggy.*

[21] Abel Heywood and Sons: op.cit.

[22] Ibid.; Winston Kime, *The Book of Skegness.*

[23] Winston Kime: *Skeggy*, taken from *Memorials of Old Lincolnshire* by E H R Tatham, 1910.

Part 2: Skegness 1653 to 1872

People

Skegness Parish Register: 1653 to 1812

The rector of the parish of Skegness kept records of baptisms and burials from 1653 onwards. There is also a record of marriages for the early part of the period. A copy of the records between 1653 and 1812 is kept in Skegness Library.[24] The table in Annex 2 analyses the information on baptisms and burials in arbitrary 10-year periods between 1653 and 1812. This information is based on individual entries in the register.[25]

Overall trends

Over the 151-year period,[*] there were 368 baptisms and 300 burials. *Prima facie* this would indicate a growing population. However, the figures take no account of inward or outward migration. The only Census figures available for the period covered by this register are for 1801 and 1811. These show a small decrease of the population of Skegness from 134 in 1801 to 132 in 1811. The crude annual figures from the registry, on the other hand, would indicate an increase in population over the same period: the figures for the years 1802 to 1811 show 37 baptisms and only 24 burials. These burials include four unidentified corpses washed up and one drowned sailor, four of whom, at least, were obviously not Skegness residents. Clearly, therefore, crude estimates of trends have to be treated with some caution.

---

[24] *An exact copy of the Skegness Parish Register 1653 to 1812*: BL. SKEG. 929. 3/1.
[25] While the records of burials should be accurate, subject to possible clerical errors, including those on the part of the present researcher, the records for baptisms *may* be understated, in the very early years. A footnote to the copy of the Register explains: "In 1644 for the first time ministers were ordered to record births as well as baptisms. In 1653 a fee of 4d. was ordered to be paid for every register of birth and burial and 12d. for marriage certificates. The registers were kept by laymen 1653-1660 and as no fee was ordered for registering baptisms in many cases they omitted to record them."
[*] The records for 1700 to 1708 have been lost.

It is, however, interesting to note – though it may be coincidental – that the total baptisms for the 70-year period from 1732 to 1801 is 200.[26] When the 49 children who died during this period are subtracted, then the figure of 151 is only a little higher than the Census figure for 1801 of 134. If the same formula (total baptisms minus child burials) were applied to the 70 years for which records are available between 1654 and 1731, the total population in 1731 would have been around 90. Comparison with other population studies for this period might show whether this possible population increase is consistent with a general trend elsewhere in the country.

Child mortality

The figures for burials of children are mainly based on entries which say "son of" or "daughter of", but also include, for example, "boy drowned age 9". It is well known that in earlier times, infant mortality was higher than it is today. The figures show that just under a third of the burials were of children.

Occupations

Usually, the former occupations of men who were buried were entered in the register from 1777 onwards. These included:

Poor man/pauper	– 3;
young man	– 1;
labourer	– 3;
rector	– 1;
grazier	– 4;
shepherd	– 3;
fisherman	– 1;
publican	– 1;
sailor	– 5 (all 1804 –12).

Apart from the rector and the publican all these occupations are rural.

Women were generally described as "wife of", "spinster", "poor woman" or "widow".

---

[26] Three score years and ten has been used as the traditional age of man; at this period it was probably lower than this.

Information is also provided of the occupations of the fathers of children baptised between 1800 and 1812. These show 25 children fathered by labourers, 8 by graziers, 4 by publicans (including 2 illegitimate children (same mother)), 1 each by a shepherd, a fisherman and a sojourning soldier.

Names

The most common surnames featuring in the earlier part of the register are: Chapman, Dyan (or Dyon), Hudson, Porter, Thompson, Warner, Whitlam (or Whitelamb), Waterman and Wilkinson.

Churchwardens' surnames between 1672 and 1744 were: Green, Whitelamb, Chapman (3), Wright, Dyon, Cotman, Bowrin, Lawrence, Barnaby, Martin, Enderby, Weldale, Everington.

A sad tale

There was no doubt a scandal in Skegness in 1674, which, unfortunately, appears to have had a sad ending.[27]

The marriage register for 1674/5 shows: "Thomas Whitelamb and Ann Hudson marry'd Apr. 27".

The baptism register for the same year shows: "William son of Thomas Whitelamb and Anne his wife baptized May the 31".

The burial register for 1674/75 shows: "Willm son of Tho : Whitelamb and An his wif. bury'd Jan 15th".

The register was signed by Tho : Thompson Rector and Tho : Whitelamb Churchwarden.

Information taken from the Census

In 1801, with 23 houses and a population of 134, Skegness was smaller than the neighbouring Wainfleet All Saints (population 506), Wainfleet St. Mary's (population 421) and Winthorpe (40 houses and a population of 221).[28]

---

[27] Ruth Neller has commented, however, that it was quite common in pre-Victorian times for couples to find out whether they could have children, before deciding to get married [personal comment given to Skegness U3A Local History Group, 9 February 2005].

[28] Winston Kime: *Skeggy*, op.cit.

By the time of the Census of 1841, Skegness had a population of 316, of whom only 28 were born outside Skegness. At that time Skegness was still a very rural community. The vast majority of the working population worked as Farmers (12), Agricultural Labourers (24) or Shepherds (2) on the dozen or so farms. There were also 17 males and 30 females listed as Servants.

Skegness had one Butcher, Grocer, Shoemaker, Bricklayer, Sweep, Attorney, Nurse, Chemist, Parish Clerk and School Teacher. There were also the Lifeboat Keeper and three Fishermen as well as two Innkeepers, a Governess, a Housekeeper, a Customs Official and a Carrier.

In 1818 only four people in Skegness were entitled to vote in the parliamentary election. In 1832, the number had increased to seven.[29]

The population of Skegness did not increase significantly between 1841 and 1871, by which time it had reached 349 *(see Annex 1)*.

Land, Buildings, Transport and Amenities

Land and Sea

A new sea defence was built east of and parallel to Roman Bank in 1670. The land in between was reclaimed.[30]

The land came into the hands of the ancestors of the Earl of Scarbrough in 1690.[31] According to Whites Directory, in 1856, Lord Monson was lord of the manor, though a great part of the soil belonged to the Earl of Scarbrough.[32]

In November 1810, there was widespread flooding, with damage to Skegness sea banks.[33] Similarly, on the night of August 30th 1833, a violent storm arrived: several vessels and many lives were lost. The

---

[29] Ruth Neller: *op. cit.*
[30] *Ibid.*
[31] G.H.J. Dutton: *Scrapbooks*, op. cit.
[32] William White: op.cit.
[33] Ruth Neller: op. cit.

lifeboat saved ten lives and 15 to 20 bodies were washed ashore in the neighbourhood.[34]

In 1829, Oldfield wrote:

> This part of the Lincolnshire coast is thought to have extended formerly to a sand called Dowsing … The parish at present contains 1630 acres of land and a border along the sea coast, in a state of waste, which is not rated. The land is of excellent quality and is well adopted for the feeding of sheep; from its contiguity to the sea, water is occasionally brackish and consequently dangerous to horned cattle. The pastures are universally fenced by ditches, there being scarcely a quickset hedge in the parish.

He went on to describe the ditches, which divided the fields as wide and dangerous and, with no trees or hedges, the place was "altogether destitute of shelter".[35]

In 1845, Skegness was described as having "rich alluvial soil yielding abundant crops of grass … when converted to tillage, the products were equally strong and good".[36]

Buildings

In 1772, Joseph Dickinson advertised the Skegness Hotel, later the Vine, as "standing on as clean a shore as any in England". Already in 1784, a bathing machine and post-chaise were available at the hotel. In 1813, New Hotel, later called Hildred's, was being advertised with seawater baths and bathing machines. In 1820, the Skegness Hotel was described as "well known for the resort of fashionable company". In 1828, the Skegness Hotel changed its name to Enderby's Hotel and in 1851 it was called the Vine Hotel. In 1862, Hobson Dunkley built the Sea View Hotel. His daughter managed it.[37]

---

[34] William White: op.cit.

[35] Winston Kime: *Skeggy*, quoting from Edmund Oldfield: *A Topographical and Historical Account of Wainfleet*, 1829.

[36] Ruth Neller: op. cit.

[37] *Ibid.*

Around 1780, McKinley House, also known as Moat House, was built in Drummond Road, not far from where the old Arcadia theatre was subsequently built.[38] This was described in an advertisement in the *Stamford Mercury* in 1810 as "a most commodious house with accommodation for a family, stables, coach-house and grass for horses". It was further claimed to command the finest sea view with the most safe and desirous bathing on the Lincolnshire coast. The Moat House was demolished towards the end of the nineteenth century. [39]

Around 1836, a Primitive Methodist Chapel was built on Roman Bank, north of the present Seathorne Methodist Church.[40] The Wesleyan Methodists erected a chapel in the High Street in 1837. In 1848, a larger Wesleyan Chapel was built, possibly out of wood, nearer to the present railway station.[41]

A Penny School opened on the west side of Roman Bank, on the site of the present School Cottages[42]. It was said to be not very good. In 1850, the Penny School building was enlarged, but it was still described as a "poking little hole".[43]

The first Skegness Post Office was opened in the High Street in 1870.[44]

Transport and Amenities

In the 1790s, a diligence ran from Skegness to Boston on Sundays and Thursdays and daily during the summer season. In 1848, the East Lincolnshire Railway opened with a station at Burgh. A horse-drawn omnibus from Skegness met the trains twice daily.[45]

---

[38] Winston Kime: *The Book of Skegness,* pp. 20-21.
[39] Ruth Neller*: op. cit.*
[40] This was called the Bank Chapel. It was demolished in the 1920's [Winston Kime, pers. comm.].
[41] Winston Kime: *The Book of Skegness*, p. 70.
[42] Mr. Kime has commented "School Cottages are on the left of School Passage (no name plate), proceeding from Roman Bank to reach Cavendish Road opposite the Infants School and could well have been the site of that first Skegness school."
[43] Winston Kime: *The Book of Skegness*, p. 77.
[44] Ruth Neller: *op. cit*.
[45] *Ibid.*

There was horse racing on the north beach at least from 1829.[46]

In 1842, Skegness is recorded as being used as a port, with over 6000 tons of coal being landed there each summer.[47]

In White's Directory, in 1826, the village of Skegness is described "as an excellent bathing place, where there are two large inns for the accommodation of visitors".[48] An anonymous writer in 1827 said: "for a place where ease and quiet can be obtained at reasonable expense, few places can compare with Skegness."[49] White's Directory, in 1856, describes Skegness as a pleasant village and bathing place. It has in its parish 1644 acres of land and 366 inhabitants. A lifeboat and bathing machines are stationed on the beach.[50]

---

[46] Ruth Neller: *op. cit.*
[47] *Ibid.*
[48] White's Directory, 1826, entry for "Wainfleet".
[49] Winston Kime: *Skeggy*, quoting from *The Lincoln and Lincolnshire Cabinet*, 1827.
[50] William White: *op. cit.*, 1856.

Part 3: Skegness 1873 to 1939

Transport

The Railway

Skegness changed forever in 1873, when the East Lincolnshire Railway Company opened a branch line to Skegness. One Saturday in September of that year, 2000 trippers (6 times the population of Skegness) arrived by train. By mid-day, the shops and refreshment rooms had run out of food. In 1881, 195,671 people arrived in Skegness by rail; in 1882, the figure was 230,277, in 1883 it was 213,299 and in 1884 it was 224,225. In 1885, the last year for which these figures are given, the number fell to 118,473.[51]

In July 1882, 17 excursion trains brought people in to watch horse racing on the north beach. On August Bank Holiday 1882 more than 20,000 visitors came by train to Skegness, the record number for a single day. Again, it is recorded that by lunchtime that day all the shops had run out of food. The last train taking the visitors home departed after 2 a.m.[52]

In 1883, the "Skegness Herald" deplored the arrival of "shoals of labourers" on the Sabbath.[53]

The Great Northern Railway took over the East Lincolnshire Railway in 1896. In 1904, the Council asked the railway company, without success, to defer the arrival of Sunday passenger trains until after the morning service. The *Jolly Fisherman* poster was first used in 1908. It was produced by the Great Northern Railway to advertise day trips from London King's Cross to Skegness. An original is kept in Skegness Town Hall. A day trip from King's Cross cost three shillings (15p).[54]

---

[51] Ruth Neller: *op. cit.*

[52] Information taken from the display in the Church Farm Museum in the summer of 2004.

[53] Ruth Neller: *op. cit.*

[54] Winston Kime: *The Book of Skegness*, p.50, and personal comment.

Buses

In 1895, Bill Berry opened a cycle shop in the High Street. It later became High Street Motor Engineers. By 1910, a charabanc had already replaced the horse-drawn bus service from the Lion Hotel to the Royal Oak at Winthorpe. In 1922, Bill Berry started a town bus service. He sold the bus company to Tom Cary in 1925. Around 1924, Stinson's Skegness Motor Service Company also began to run buses in Skegness. Charles Atkin, Tom Cary, R.C.F. Chown, E.C. Raynor (Chapel St. Leonards) and others operated buses to nearby villages, with Underwood's open top double-decker buses providing a regular service to Boston. In the season, penny-all-the-way 'toast racks' ran between the Clock Tower and the Sea View Hotel.[55] A bus station was built on Drummond Road in 1937.[56]

The Layout of the Town

Up to 1873, only two roads existed. One was the present narrow and winding High Street. The other was Roman Bank, from which a road went down to the sea by the Sea View Hotel.[57]

Two or three years after the railway reached Skegness in 1873, the Earl of Scarbrough commissioned Wainfleet surveyor, G.B. Walker to draw up a plan for the layout of the new town of Skegness.[58] The plan shows Grand Promenade, Rutland Road, Lumley Road and Roman Bank and the projected position of the Pier. New roads were to be Lumley Avenue, Algitha Road and Ida Road, Scarbrough Avenue, Lilian Road, Sibell Road and Osbert Road. The first four were built under the guidance of Mr H. Tippett, the entrepreneurial agent of the Earl of Scarbrough. Lilian Road and Sibell Road were planned to be located – running east and west – between Scarbrough Avenue and what was later to be Castleton

---

[55] Winston Kime: *The Book of Skegness*, p.106.
[56] Ruth Neller: *op. cit.*
[57] *The Pier: op. cit.*
[58] Winston Kime [pers. comm.], citing Albert Thompson's *Skegness Pier* (1989) (see also *The Book of Skegness*, p.32).

Boulevard. This was to be called Osbert Road, but it was not constructed until 1934.[59]

In 1877 work began on building a sea wall from north of Sea View Lane to Derby Avenue. The Grand and South Parades were built on the western side of this wall. By 1878, Skegness had developed sufficiently for its streetlights to be visible from the sea. By 1880, most of the planned plots on Lumley Road had been sold and, by 1882, it was almost built up.[60]

The newly formed Skegness Pier Company commissioned Clarke and Pickerell in about 1880 to design the pier. It was completed in 1881.[61] The Gothic style entrance was retained until 1937, when a contemporary style replacement was built with balustrades on the twin ramps. This lasted until 1972, when it was replaced by the present structure. In 1898, a Venetian Fair was held on the pier with illuminated boats; the pier was decorated with twinkling lights. [62] On the morning of 21st March 1919 a 200-ton schooner 'Europa' of Amsterdam dragged its anchor on spring tides and, at 8 o'clock, it was swept out of control towards the pier. This was the biggest disaster, which had ever happened to the pier superstructure up to that date, as the vessel lurched into the sides of the pier irons, cutting the deck completely in half and crashing through, eventually going aground on the south side. It was twenty years before the damage was repaired. In the meantime, a temporary gangway was constructed around the two halves so people could still walk to the pier head.[63]

The fountain, now in the Fairy Dell, was originally situated in Lumley Square, and was moved into Marine Gardens (now the site of the Embassy building) in 1888.

---

[59] Winston Kime [pers. comm.].

[60] Ruth Neller: *op. cit.*

[61] Winston Kime [pers. comm.].

[62] Ruth Neller: *op. cit.*

[63] It was, of course, only minor damage, compared to the disaster of 1978 (Winston Kime [pers. comm.]).

In 1898, Skegness Urban District Council (UDC) leased the area between the high and low water mark from the Board of Trade. In 1922, Skegness UDC purchased the foreshore, west of the high tide mark, from the Earl of Scarbrough. [64]

The Clock Tower was erected in 1899 to celebrate Queen Victoria's Diamond Jubilee. [65]

In 1912 Rowland Henry Jenkins became town surveyor and engineer. He remained in post until he retired in 1952. In 1922, he prepared plans to develop the foreshore area into a holiday playground. The Tower Esplanade was completed in 1923. The Boating Lake opened in 1924, the first major work in the Skegness Urban District Council's original foreshore development plan. The lake was doubled in size in 1930. His scheme for the development of the North Foreshore was put into effect around 1930. This included the waterway, tennis courts, bowling greens and walks. In 1938, the waterway was extended southward to Tower Esplanade. [66]

In 1928, the bathing pool, the Embassy ballroom, restaurant and orchestral piazza were opened.[67]

The first municipal car park opened in the former Marine Gardens in 1928.[68]

In 1930, Scarbrough Avenue was finally metalled and kerbed.[69]

The Sun Castle was opened in 1932 as a solarium with ultra-violet ray lamps for artificial sunbathing, but it did not catch on. The lamps were eventually removed and, under the efficient management of Mrs. Hanson, it became a popular spot for light refreshment and soft music.[70]

---

[64] Ruth Neller: *op. cit.*

[65] *Ibid.*

[66] *Ibid.*

[67] *Ibid.*

[68] *Ibid.*

[69] *Ibid.*

[70] Winston Kime: *Skeggy.*

Lumley Square in 1920 was very much a horse and cart thoroughfare.[71] In 1934 it was reconstructed, with a gas office and public toilets replacing old cottages.[72]

Castleton Boulevard was opened in 1934, bringing the first traffic lights to the town.[73] It was going to be called "Castleton Road", but, apparently, councillors went to Paris, shortly before it was due to be opened, and, after seeing the boulevards there, they decided that "Castleton Boulevard" sounded better.

Sea View Lane was changed to Sea View Road in comparatively recent times, the change taking place without any announcement.[74]

Local Government and Public Services

Until 1885 the "Skegness Parish Vestry" administered Skegness.

In 1883, the Skegness Parish Vestry purchased the resort's first fire engine.[75]

A Local Government Board was elected in 1885 to take over the running of Skegness from the Parish Vestry. In the same year, Skegness became part of the newly-formed Horncastle division for parliamentary elections. In 1895, Skegness became an Urban District Council (UDC). In 1926, Winthorpe became part of the UDC.[76]

Police and Law courts

In 1908, Skegness was allocated its own petty sessional court. It functioned only in the summer. In 1929, a new courthouse was built on Roman Bank, next to the police Headquarters. It was used all the year round. In 1931, Skegness became the divisional police Headquarters for the Spilsby, Alford and Mablethorpe area.[77]

---

[71] Winston Kime: *Skegness in the 1920's & 30's*, L.SKEG.909
[72] Ruth Neller: *op. cit.*
[73] *Ibid.*
[74] Winston Kime [pers. comm.].
[75] Ruth Neller: *op. cit.*
[76] I*bid.*
[77] *Ibid.*

Library Service
From 1929, the County Library Service was run by volunteers from the old High Street Labour Exchange, 2 evenings weekly. The County Library Service moved to the Town Hall, which had been rebuilt by that time, in 1931.[78]

Public Utilities

In 1877 a Gas Company was formed. The gasworks were built at a cost of £3,500.[79] A sanitary system was arranged in the same year.

Waterworks were constructed in 1879.[80] In 1904, the Earl of Scarbrough had a borehole sunk at Welton Le Marsh, with a reservoir and water main to increase the water supply. The Urban District Council bought the water company from the Earl of Scarbrough for £40,000 in 1909.[81] The soft pure water from the boreholes at Welton had only 5 degrees of hardness.[82]

Both the gas and waterworks were extended in the 1920s. In 1927, a concrete water tower was built on Burgh Road to replace a smaller brick one.[83] The new water tower was a landmark, for many years, along with the gasholder. By 1935, the Urban District Council had acquired ownership of the gas works.[84]

The Mid-Lincolnshire Electricity Supply Company supplied mains electricity in 1932.[85]

A large sewage disposal works was built on Burgh Marsh in 1936.[86]

[78] Ruth Neller: *op. cit.*
[79] *Ibid.*
[80] *The Pier, op. cit.*
[81] Ruth Neller: *op. cit.*
[82] *Skegness Guide*, 1935
[83] Ruth Neller: *op. cit.*
[84] *Skegness Guide, op. cit.*
[85] Ruth Neller: *op. cit.*
[86] *Ibid.*

Public Buildings

Churches and Chapels

The foundation stone of St. Matthew's Church was laid in 1879.[87] The Earl of Scarbrough donated the site, plus £3,000. The "living" was in the gift of the Earl. The stipend was £240 per annum.[88] The nave and south aisle were consecrated in 1880. The north aisle and chancel were completed in 1885 and the final consecration performed. The Lord Lieutenant unveiled a War Memorial on the south side of the church in 1923. The choir vestry was added to St. Matthews' Church in 1935.[89]

A third Wesleyan chapel was opened in 1876 in the High Street. The second one (near the railway station – *see Part 2*) was demolished. A larger Wesleyan chapel was built on Algitha Road in 1882. The Wesleyan Manse was built on Lumley Avenue in 1899. A smaller Manse was provided for Wesleyan ministers in 1935.[90]

A new Primitive Methodist chapel was built on the west side of Roman Bank in 1881, costing £327.[91] In 1899 they built another new chapel on the east side of Roman Bank, at a cost, with the Sunday School, of £2040. (This is now a second-hand furniture shop.) In 1924, a church parlour was added to the rear of this chapel and a war memorial was fixed on the wall.[92]

---

[87] Ruth Neller: *op. cit.*

[88] Abel Heywood and Sons: *op. cit.*

[89] Ruth Neller: *op. cit.*

[90] *Ibid.*

[91] Winston Kime has pointed out [pers. comm.] that you can see this chapel if you walk along School Passage towards Roman Bank: "at the rear of the Roman Bank terrace houses you will see one with rounded sash windows edged by red stained glass. This was the first Primitive Methodist Chapel in the town area".

[92] Winston Kime: *The Book of Skegness* and pers. comm. Mr Kime adds "As far as I know, the war memorial plaque to the half dozen PM members who died is still on the exterior west wall, but it has been boarded off and obscured from view. Several years ago, when the screen was put up, I wrote to the then Methodist minister suggesting they remove the plaque and refix in the entrance vestibule of the present Skegness Methodist Church. He replied that he would report the matter to his next meeting of the trustees. I heard nothing more and do not know if the plaque is still there, although I pass within a few yards of where it should be almost every day!"

The inaugural meeting of Skegness Baptist Church was held in 1894 in a "tin tabernacle" in Beresford Avenue. St. Paul's Baptist Church, built in brick, also in Beresford Avenue was opened in 1911.[93] Before then, what is now Beresford Avenue was only a rough cart track leading up to garden nurseries and greenhouses and on to Drummond Road. As the land was developed, it was paved, surfaced and named.[94]

The first Roman Catholic Church was opened in 1898 in Grosvenor Road and dedicated to the Sacred Heart. It cost £500 and had seating for 500. A new church on an adjoining site in Grosvenor Road was consecrated in 1950.[95]

In 1913, the Salvation Army established a separate corps in Skegness. The Salvation Army Citadel opened on the High Street in 1929.[96] This citadel was demolished and replaced by the present building, slightly to the west of the present site, in 1995.[97]

Skegness and District Cottage Hospital

The first building

A meeting was held in 1906 or 1907 to consider a proposal for a Skegness hospital, but it did not materialise due to lack of support.

The project was discussed again in 1911, the year of the Coronation of George V. It was first mentioned in the *Skegness News* on 15 March of that year and, on 17 March, Councillor Samuel Moody, Chairman of Skegness Urban District Council, presided a first public meeting. Wards for males and females were to cost £1,000. It was anticipated that income would exceed expenditure by £100 per year. The first officers were: Drs. A.W. Allan, Benjamin Sweeten and Stanley Wallace.

On 18 March, the local Member of Parliament, Captain A.G. Weigall (later Lt. Col. Sir Archibald Weigall, KCMG)

---

[93] Ruth Neller: *op. cit.*
[94] Winston Kime [pers. comm.].
[95] Winston Kime: *The Book of Skegness*, p. 69.
[96] Ruth Neller: *op. cit.*
[97] Winston Kime [pers. comm.].

promised to give £250 to funds, provided that an additional £250 was raised by Coronation Day on 22 June.

At a further meeting on 31 March, the Earl of Scarbrough agreed to give a site: 1700 square yards of approved land to the value of £350. Sites considered included one at the end of Coronation Walk and one in the plantation on the south side of Cecil Avenue. The committee rejected both these sites on 14 July. Instead, they chose a site on Wainfleet Road, which is the site occupied by the east front of the present hospital. Although the Earl of Scarbrough gave the site, the hospital committee had to bear the cost of making up the road in front of it (the south end of the present Dorothy Avenue). The committee were also told that Her Highness Princess Marie Louise of Schleswig-Holstein had expressed her willingness to assist the project and had promised to lay the foundation stone.

She laid the foundation stone on 29 September 1911. This was a great day in the history of the resort and all Skegness turned out for the occasion. The ceremony took place in a field on the north side of Wainfleet Road, a field which was then surrounded by trees, but which became part of the site of the present hospital. It was agreed that the hospital should be considered to be a permanent memorial of the Coronation of King George V and the public procession to and from the hospital site was to rival in size and colour the Coronation Procession, which had taken place on 22 June. The stone was fashioned hollow. After she had laid it, the Princess placed in its cavity an airtight leaden casket containing a copy of the programme signed by Her Highness, current issues of *The Times* and two local newspapers – the *Skegness News* and *Skegness Herald* – together with some coins of the year. Forty-three children presented to Her Highness purses containing money for the hospital fund, totalling £56. After tea, taken in marquees in the grounds, the Princess inspected the Fire Brigade, the Lifeboat Crew, Boy Scouts' troops and Boys' Brigade companies. Later, the units paraded back to the Clock Tower, until they were dismissed after the playing of the National Anthem.

A three-day Bazaar raised £533 in the Pleasure Gardens (now the Tower Gardens) on 14, 15 and 16 August 1912.

The Opening Ceremony was held on Monday 19 May 1913. The units, which had been on parade at the "Stone laying", were there again but with some changes: the 1st Skegness Boys' Brigade Company had become the 1st Company of the 3rd Lincoln Cadet Battalion. The Senior Boy Scout Troop had transformed itself into a Sea Scout Unit and they and their Scoutmaster had gone into Navalized Uniform. Representatives of the Territorial Army and of the Lincolnshire Yeomanry also attended in uniform. The total cost of the building was £1450. Towards this, £1000 had already been received in subscriptions and donations and a further £200 was available from the balance of the proceeds of the bazaar. This left a deficit of £250. Named Dorothy Avenue, the access road to the site had become the first stretch of the present Dorothy Avenue, on the west side of which the diminutive hospital was set like a jewel. Mr. F.J. Parkinson of Blackburn – the successful architect in a competition, for which 56 firms had entered – presented Lady Scarbrough with the key to the hospital. Miss Mollie Sweeten presented her with a bouquet.

A miniature hospital, it had three single bedded wards, a bathroom etc., a small operating theatre annex and a sterilising room. It also had a storeroom, matron's room, kitchens and out offices on the ground floor. On the first floor there were three bedrooms for the matron, nurses and servant, with a bathroom etc. and a storeroom. It was noted that "enlargement can be made without disturbance to the original building".

The first new wing

Soon there was need for a larger operating theatre. The hospital received a "windfall" – a bequest of £516 from the late Mr. Fred Ingle. This facilitated the new wing and ward. Messrs. Geo. Dunkley and Son of Skegness secured the contract at £455. This brought the accommodation up to eight beds, one cot and a private ward. The extension opened on 1 July 1915. A mortuary was built the same year at a cost of £45, while the Earl of Scarbrough presented a revolving roof shelter.

Extensions in the 1920s

By 1920, funds for a further extension had grown to £818. It was decided, however, that three-quarters of the estimated cost should be in hand before work was commenced. The further extension was undertaken in 1922. This comprised an additional ward, a ward kitchen, two nurses' rooms, six extra beds and two more private wards. The cost, including the installation of hot water pipes and radiators in the public wards, was £1688. These additions brought accommodation to 15 beds and a cot in all. Hospital President, the Earl of Scarbrough, accompanied by his only daughter, Lady Serena, unveiled the tablet in the Memorial Ward to the memory of the Skegness men who fell in World War I.

The porters' lodge was completed in 1925.

A hot and cold water supply was installed in the operating theatre in 1926 at a cost of £24.

Extensions in the 1930s

An appeal was launched in 1929 for an X-Ray installation. On 22 September 1931, Mrs. V.P. Druce[98] of Seacroft formally opened a new operating theatre, an X-Ray Department and additional staff accommodation.[99]

By 1934 in-patients had risen to a then record total of 391 in the year, emphasising the necessity of increasing the bed capacity with as little delay as possible. Plans were considered for two new wards and the conversion of existing buildings to administrative and staff use. A minimum outlay of £7,000 was anticipated. In 1935, plans

---

[98] Mrs. Druce was the wife of Colonel Druce, then secretary of Seacroft Golf Club [Winston Kime, pers. comm.].
[99] It was noted: "a suitable X-ray installation has been purchased and will be in actual use as soon as a town supply of electricity is available". Mid-Lincolnshire Electricity Supply came in 1932.

were prepared for an ambitious scheme for a new hospital building and for the conversion of the existing premises at a cost of £20,000, including furnishings and equipment. However, only £315 remained in the building fund at the time. The full scheme was deferred and in 1936 it was decided to concentrate on the £7,000 section for which the need was most pressing. Amended plans in 1937 were for a £15,600 scheme, which included new male and female wards and a separate maternity block.[100] These were completed in 1939. [101]

Other Medical Facilities

The Nottinghamshire Convalescent Home was built in 1891 on Seathorne sand hills. The Derbyshire Poor Children's Home opened in Scarbrough Avenue in the same year.[102] The National Deposit Friendly Society's Memorial Convalescent Home was opened in 1927.[103] Carey House women's convalescent home opened in 1933.[104]

By 1935, the St. John's Ambulance and the Red Cross had been established.[105]

The Town Hall

In 1920, the UDC bought the Earl of Scarbrough's estate office at the junction of Roman Bank and Algitha Road for £3000. The estate office moved to the former Council Office at 23, Algitha Road. The estate office moved again in the 1930's – to the Hall on Roman Bank. In 1928, the Council offices on Roman Bank were destroyed by fire. Many town records were lost. The first Town Hall was built on the site of the burned-out offices in 1931.[106] In 1964, the Council acquired a new Town Hall - the former National Deposit Friendly

---

[100] The whole of the above section was taken from *Skegness and District Hospital 1913-1963 – Golden Jubilee.*
[101] Ruth Neller: *op. cit.*
[102] *Ibid.*
[103] Winston Kime: *Skeggy.*
[104] Ruth Neller: *op. cit.*
[105] *Skegness Guide*, 1935
[106] Ruth Neller: *op. cit.*

Society's Memorial Convalescent Home, which by then had been closed because the introduction of the National Health Service had caused its membership to fall drastically.[107]

The Post Office

In 1888, the Post Office moved to Lumley Road. In 1905, it moved to the corner of Algitha Road and became the General Post Office. (This is now Lloyds TSB bank.) In 1929, a new General Post Office and telephone exchange was built on Roman Bank to replace it. [108]

Schools

A new, larger, Skegness National school was opened on Roman Bank in 1880. A County Council Infants' School opened in Cavendish Road in 1908. A junior school was added in 1935. [109]

Near the end of the nineteenth century and the early twentieth century, Skegness had a number of private boarding schools. The Essendon Girls' School was at the north end of Rutland Terrace, now the Masonic Hall. There was at least one other smaller private boarding school further along Rutland Terrace on Rutland Road. Brythwen High School, established in 1899, is now the Lyndhurst Club on the corner of Lumley Avenue and Algitha Road.

Between the wars, the private Orient Girls' School was located in what are now the Charnwood Hotel and the New Park Club. Leeson Lodge, the large bungalow next to the latter was the Orient Preparatory School for Boys, earlier based in Algitha Road. Mr. and Mrs. Boyer owned the Orient schools or colleges. The Inglewood Preparatory School was in Ida Road, under the two Miss Sweetens, daughters of Dr. Benjamin Sweeten, whose house and surgery was next door, in Lumley Avenue. The Seacroft Preparatory School for Boys was a boarding school on Seacroft Esplanade, now a nursing home. The proprietor was H.E. Sparrow. Consequently, it was usually known as Sparrow's School. The boys wore bright red

---

[107] Winston Kime: *Skeggy* and pers. comm..
[108] Ruth Neller: *op. cit.*
[109] Winston Kime: *The Book of Skegness*, pp. 77-79.

school caps and it specialised in training boys for the Royal Navy. Mr. Sparrow was, for a number of years, honorary secretary of the local lifeboat. The school closed at the outbreak of World War II and was later taken over by the RAF Recruit Centre as a sick bay. After the war it was for several years the Seacroft Special School for Girls.[110]

In 1932, Lumley Secondary Modern School opened in Pelham Road. It was demolished in 1993. It was supplemented in 1957 by the Morris Secondary School, Church Road, now incorporated in St. Clement's College.[111]

In 1933, Skegness Grammar School replaced Magdalen College School, Wainfleet as the main Grammar School in the area. Before that, well over half the pupils at Magdalen College travelled from Skegness by train each day. The next nearest grammar schools were at Spilsby and Alford.[112]

Skegness Beam Wireless Station

The skyline to the north of Skegness completely changed in the spring of 1926. It was early April of that year when eight masts were completed; they were of a lattice construction 287 feet in height, five times taller than the Clock Tower.[113]

The first mast closest to Skegness was just to the north of Burgh Road only 150 yards from the Water Works. The next four masts were set in a straight line, the remaining three were at right angles with the last one, which was a quarter of a mile west of Winthorpe Church.

These masts were strung out covering a length of one and a half miles, and along with the control building (now converted into a bungalow) on Church Lane helped to link India and Australia by wireless to Britain.

---

[110] Winston Kime [pers. comm.].
[111] Ruth Neller: *op. cit.*
[112] Winston Kime [pers. comm.].
[113] This section is taken from cuttings from *Skegness News*, 1927 to 1938, L.SKEG.384.

The GPO erected the masts. The operating company was "The Imperial and International Communications Ltd."

Communications commenced the following year. On 13 April 1927 the Secretary of State for the Colonies, Mr. L.S. Amery, sent a message from London through Skegness to Mr. Bruce, the Prime Minister of Australia, who replied the next day by wireless through Skegness, then by landline to London, a total of 10,000 miles.

The results of the 1931 Derby were telegraphed around the world in record time. From the time that the winning horse "Cameronian" passed the post to the result reaching Bombay and Alexandria was two seconds, for Cape Town and Hong Kong it was three seconds, for Australia four seconds and for South America only five seconds.

The station was in use for 12 years. During the autumn of 1938 it was decided that the masts would be dismantled within the next two years. The reason given was that Cable and Wireless Ltd were "centralising their services". In fact, all eight masts were removed during the early part of 1940 when they had become a hazard to aircraft.

Hotels and Amenities

Hotels

As previously indicated, there were three hotels in Skegness prior to the arrival of the railway: The Vine, Hildreds and the Sea View Hotel.

The Lumley Hotel opened on Good Friday 1880. The Lion Hotel opened at the corner of Lumley Road and Roman Bank in 1881.[114] It had a stone lion on the roof, which was was carved by Richard Winn of Grimsby and weighed about six hundredweight. The stone lion was removed from the roof of the Lion Hotel in 1904, when it became unsafe. It remained on the pavement outside until recent times, when the national brewery company, who took over the hotel, unceremoniously removed it.

---

[114] Ruth Neller: *op. cit.*; Winston Kime [pers. comm.].

The Hydro (Hotel) opened as a health establishment in 1900. It later changed its name to the Seacroft Hotel.[115]

A new frontage up to the North Parade was built on to the Sea View Hotel in 1911. Some eight years later, the west end of the hotel was converted into flats.[116]

Billy Lambe converted Gomersall House into the Marine Hotel in 1920. Fred Walker built the Imperial Hotel and Ballroom in 1930. The County Hotel opened in 1935. In the same year a 12-bedroomed guesthouse on Castleton Boulevard was put up for sale for £1,750.[117]

In 1927 a public referendum was held and voted in favour of Sunday opening of eating-places. In 1932, the UDC gave approval for Sunday trading across the board, subject to compliance with the law.[118]

In 1936, the Ship Hotel, on the northwest corner of Roman Bank and Burgh Road, was demolished.[119]

Holiday Camps and Holiday Homes

A holiday home for Nottingham girls opened in Brunswick Drive in 1912. In 1928, Nottingham poor children's holiday home opened in Roseberry Avenue, after several years in tents and huts.[120]

In the 1920s the first tent and caravan parks came into fashion. The YMCA set up a canvas camp in Grosvenor Road. In 1930, this camp became the Woodside Holiday Centre.[121]

In 1936, Billy Butlin opened Skegness Luxury Holiday Camp at Ingoldmells. There were two big fires at the camp in one week in 1939.

The Derbyshire Miners' Welfare Holiday Camp in Winthorpe Avenue opened in 1936.[122]

---

[115] Ruth Neller: *op. cit.*
[116] *Ibid.*
[117] *Ibid.*
[118] *Ibid.*
[119] *Ibid.*
[120] *Ibid.*
[121] *Ibid.*
[122] Winston Kime [pers. comm.].

At the outbreak of war in 1939, the Royal Navy took over Butlins camp and converted it to a training unit, known as HMS Royal Arthur. In the autumn concrete bases for six-inch guns were constructed at Jackson's corner and Gibraltar Point. The RAF requisitioned hotels, guesthouses and private residences to billet trainees at the Skegness RAF Recruit Training Centre, which opened in March 1941.[123]

Cinemas, Theatres and Dance Halls

Fred Clements opened the Arcadia Theatre in 1911. The Lawn Theatre, later the Lawn cinema, was built by Bass, owners of the Hildred's Hotel, at about the same time. It was closed in 1934 and the building was incorporated into Hildred's Hotel. Also in 1911, the Alhambra Dance Hall opened on the site of Lawrence & Bircumshaw's open air roller skating rink opposite the Figure 8 *(see below)*. A casino opened on this site in 1922. The Central Hall, on Roman Bank, which had been built as a dance hall, was converted into a cinema in 1912. Also in 1912, the Sands Pavilion opened, mainly for tea dances. It later became known as the Café Dansant. The Skegness Urban District Council set up a new foreshore department there in 1934.[124]

In 1920, the Tower and Lawn cinemas were allowed to give Sunday performances only on condition that half the profits were donated to Skegness Hospital.[125]

In 1931, Louis Henshall of the Sea View Hotel built the Winter Gardens near to the hotel, originally as a roller skating rink. The Parade cinema opened in 1933 or 1934 on the Grand Parade. Fred Clements retired in 1935 and sold the Tower and Arcadia to the owners of the new Parade cinema.[126]

---

[123] Winston Kime [pers. comm.].
[124] Ruth Neller: *op. cit.*
[125] Winston Kime: *Skeggy.*
[126] Ruth Neller: *op. cit.*

Amusements and Distractions

From 1883, the paddle steamer "May" ran trips from Skegness Pier. Other boats ran similar trips in later years.[127] Some of these paddle steamer trips went to Hunstanton, enabling people to visit Sandringham.

In 1882, warm water swimming baths were opened in Scarbrough Avenue.[128] Enemy bombs destroyed them during the Second World War.

A switchback railway was built on a large part of the Jungle frontage on North Parade in 1885. It was dismantled in about 1912. A Figure 8 railway was built on North Parade in 1908. In 1915, a joywheel ride in front of the Figure 8 was destroyed by fire.[129]

Lifeboats and fire engines were used in carnival processions as far back as 1907.

The Lincolnshire Agricultural Show was held in Skegness in 1912 and in 1922, in fields in Richmond Drive. Circuses also took place on the same site.

In 1923, the fairground was transferred from the central beach to the North Parade; it was called Pleasureland. In 1925, Billy Butlin set up stalls in the Park, across the road from Clement's Happy Valley. In 1928 he obtained permission to open his amusement park on Sunday afternoons. In 1929, all amusements on the North Parade had to be removed to avoid disturbing the National Friendly Deposit Society Home. In the same year Billy Butlin built and ran a new fairground, on a site leased from the council, south of the pier.

Skegness Town Band was formed in 1923.[130]

In 1932, the Skegness Advancement Association inaugurated the first illuminations on Lumley Road, the clock tower and the lake.[131]

In 1932, the newly formed Skegness Aero Club staged an air pageant, attracting 15,000 spectators, on the Royal Oak aerodrome,

---

[127] Ruth Neller: *op. cit.*

[128] *Ibid.*

[129] *Ibid.*

[130] Ruth Neller: *op. cit.*

[131] *Ibid.*

Roman Bank, on the north side of the hotel and Royal Oak Terrace, Winthorpe.[132]

By 1935, there were two social clubs for residents in Skegness: The Avenue in Lumley Avenue (which is still in business) and The Tennyson in Drummond Road. Skegness Amateur Operatic Society had also been established by this time, as had the St. John's Ambulance and the Red Cross.[133]

Sports Facilities

The Cricket Ground was acquired in 1879: it was described in publicity material, a few years later, as one of the finest in the country. In 1886, the Australian Touring Eleven Cricket Team played in Skegness: 16 excursion trains ran.[134]

The first game of golf was played on Seacroft Golf Course in 1895. The course was later extended from 9 to 18 holes. The North Shore Golf Course was completed in 1910.[135]

In 1931, the first open bowls tournament was held on the north shore greens.[136]

By 1935, in addition to the two golf clubs, there were clubs for swimming, bowls, cricket, rugby, football, hockey and angling.[137]

Shops and Services

The Skegness Steam Laundry opened on Roman Bank in 1877 to meet the needs of the new hotels and lodging houses. The Fry family took over the laundry in 1928. The Hygienic Laundry opened in the 1890s on the site of the present Kwiksave supermarket.[138]

Ruth Neller: *op. cit.*; Winston Kime [pers. comm.].
[133] *Skegness Guide*, 1935
[134] Ruth Neller: *op. cit.*
[135] *Ibid.*
[136] *Ibid.*
[137] *Skegness Guide*, 1935
[138] Ruth Neller: *op. cit.*

In 1880, a cattle market opened near the railway station. This only lasted a few years. George F. Ball, an auctioneer, started a new cattle market near the gas works in 1923. This closed in 1937.[139]

In 1880, Croft's Drapery shop opened on Lumley Road. It also had a frontage on to the High Street.[140]

In 1882, no fewer than ten builders were listed in White's Directory for Skegness. In the same year, Lord Scarbrough bought Warth & Dunkley's brickworks on Wainfleet Road. John Cater opened a new brickworks, also on Wainfleet Road.[141]

The 1914 Skegness Bungalow and House Seekers Guide shows the following shops and services:

> Farmers Dairy, 20 Lumley Road
> Crofts (Drapers)
> J.T. Grey, Family Grocer, Drummond Road Stores and Post Office. (This is still a Post Office.)
> Duttons, Lumley Road
> J.T. Borman, Coal Merchant, Station Yard
> Alfred Wrate, Photographer, 17 Lumley Road
> Hiley's Restaurant (now the National Westminster Bank).[142]

Alfred Heyward's peppermint rock factory opened in 1920.[143]

In the 1920s Dutton's Stores in Lumley Road sold almost anything from books to knitting wool and had a circulating library many years before the County Library was established in Skegness. The shop opened in the early 1890's and closed in the 1960s.[144]

Woolworths "nothing over sixpence" store opened in Lumley Road in 1928.[145]

In 1930, shops were built over the front lawns of Lumley Terrace and Harrington Gardens.[146]

---

[139] Ruth Neller: *op. cit.*
[140] *Ibid.*
[141] *Ibid.*
[142] *Skegness Bungalow and House Seekers Guide*, 1914
[143] Ruth Neller: *op. cit.*
[144] Winston Kime: *Skeggy.*
[145] Ruth Neller: *op. cit.*

Newspapers

The first edition of the *Skegness Herald* appeared in 1882, edited and printed by John Avery. In 1909, the first edition of the *Skegness News* appeared, published by Charles Henry Major. In 1915, Major took over the *Skegness Herald*. In 1917, the latter ceased publication. The Boston-based *Lincolnshire Standard* launched the *Skegness Standard* in 1922.[147]

Housing

The first council houses – 100 – were built in Skegness in 1920 on Marsh Lane. It then changed its name to "Richmond Drive".[148]

In 1935, a small three-bedroomed semi-detached house on Wainfleet Road was put up for sale for £425.[149]

Life and Death in Skegness

The population of Skegness increased from 349 in 1871 to 1,338 in 1881. By 1901, it had reached 2,140 and by 1931, it was 9,121 (compared with 16,809 in 1991 – *see Annex 1*).

A skeleton was found in the walls of the Vine Hotel in 1902 with brass buttons. It is believed to be a Customs Officer who had disappeared years earlier.[150]

---

[146] Ruth Neller: *op. cit.*
[147] *Ibid.*
[148] *Ibid.*
[149] *Ibid.*
[150] Information taken from material on display at the Church Farm Museum, summer 2004.

Part 4: <u>The Lifeboat</u>

In 1816 a 24-pounder brass mortar was sent to Skegness coast guards to help with ship rescues.[151]

There has been a lifeboat in Skegness for over one and a half centuries. In 1825 the first lifeboat in the area was placed at Gibraltar Point. This was one year after the founding of the RNLI by Sir William Hilary on 4 March 1824. The lifeboat was moved to Skegness in 1830 because it was found that, in northerly or north-easterly gales, it was too far to leeward of the sandbanks and likely to trap vessels running for the shelter of the Wash. A lifeboat house was built in the sand dunes at what is now known as Lifeboat Avenue.[152] A new and bigger lifeboat house was built in South Parade in 1864.[153] In 1892, the Lifeboat Station was rebuilt on the same site.[154]

The first lifeboat was installed and maintained by the Lincolnshire Coast Shipwreck Association, which was formed in 1826 and amalgamated with RNLI in 1863. The Lincolnshire Shipwreck Association was wound up in 1911, when the RNLI took over completely.[155]

Herbert Ingram II was the third Skegness Lifeboat in service, from 1874 to 1888. The widow of Herbert Ingram, Boston, paid for it. He was an MP and founder of *The Illustrated London News*. He perished in a shipping disaster on Lake Michigan. The last sailing lifeboat was decommissioned in 1932, when the first motor lifeboat, "Anne Allen", was launched.[156]

---

[151] Ruth Neller: *op. cit.*
[152] *Ibid.*
[153] *Ibid.*
[154] *Ibid.*
[155] *Ibid.*
[156] *Ibid.*

Part 5: Winthorpe

The Parish of Winthorpe is mentioned in the Doomsday Book. It was bounded on the East by the Roman Bank; on the North by the villages of Ingoldmells and Addlethorpe; on the West by Burgh le Marsh and on the South by Skegness.[157]

It is now almost indistinguishable from the seaside resort of Skegness and in 1926 it became a part of the Skegness Urban District.

Professor Kenneth Cameron, in his *Dictionary of Lincolnshire Place-names*, defines "Winthorpe" as "Wine's thorpe – a secondary settlement of Skegness or Ingoldmells".[158]

The Parish contains 2,300 acres. In 1965, two thirds of the land was said to be farmed, although the holiday industry employed more people and was already far more important.

Until modern methods of drainage were introduced, the land was not suitable for arable cultivation as the land is situated below sea level and was originally in the marsh. It did, however, produce excellent grazing. It had a reputation for fattening bullocks and was keenly sought by inland farmers and graziers for finishing off their in-wintered stock.

In the reign of Elizabeth I there were 55 families living in Winthorpe. By 1881 there were 337 people and 1,650 by 1961.

The Church of St. Mary's was built in the fifteenth century on the site of an earlier church. Much of the church was spoilt, as records show, in the frenzy that possessed England in the seventeenth century. However, the bells remain. There are four bells. The oldest 'G' is 35 inches in diameter and was cast in about 1370. The treble (33.5 inches in diameter) bears the date 1595. The other

---

[157] Information taken from a hand written book prepared by members of the Winthorpe Women's Institute to celebrate the Golden Jubilee of the W.I. Movement (1915-1965) modified on the basis of personal comments by Winston Kime.

[158] Winston Kime, personal comment, based on Kenneth Cameron: *Dictionary of Lincolnshire Place-names*, English Place-name Society, 1998.

two bells were cast in 1604. In addition, there is a small bell known as "ting-tang" which was originally a Sanctus bell housed in the little cote that, from the outside, can be seen at the east end of the nave.

Church Farm House is the oldest house left in Winthorpe. It was built in 1765.

The Old Workhouse was built in 1820.

The Old School House (now the Charnwood Hotel) was built in 1865 for the education of 57 children.

In 1910, the present Seathorne Methodist Church replaced the Old Bank Chapel.[159]

The Derbyshire Miners' Convalescent Home was built in 1928.[160]

---

[159] Ruth Neller: *op. cit.*
[160] *Ibid.*

<u>Conclusion</u>

The one thing we know about Skegness up to a couple of hundred years ago is that we do not know a great deal. We know that Burgh existed in Roman times and that Wainfleet was an important, if fairly modest, port until relatively recent times. We do not know whether Skegness had any significant role to play in the development of either of these places.

There is sufficient evidence to suggest that the geography of Skegness changed drastically in the sixteenth century. The "ness" part of the name suggests that there was some sort of promontory here, which could not be said to be the case now. There is written evidence too that the previous church was washed away by the sea. There is believable evidence to suggest that there was some sort of castle or fort here too. To go further and suggest that Skegness was a thriving commercial centre or port is probably pure conjecture. There are only brief references to Skegness (Tric) in the Domesday Book. The first indication we have of the population of Skegness is in the sixteenth century, when there were fourteen families. Even at ten people per family, this would only give a population of 140 – about the same as in 1801. Nevertheless it *is* possible that Skegness was a lively port in the Middle Ages.

From the parish records of the seventeenth, eighteenth and early nineteenth century and from the early census figures, we can build up a better picture of what life might have been like in Skegness during that period. First, it was small, with a population of less than 150. Second, it was predominantly agricultural (rather than maritime): nearly all the occupations referred to in the records are related to agriculture. There was a high infant mortality rate, but probably no higher than elsewhere in the country. Many of the people would have lived in isolated farmsteads scattered around the parish. The village (or hamlet) was very small, probably centred around the present High Street, with the church out in the fields some half a mile further inland. Roman Bank and Wainfleet Road existed and there was a lane down to the sea where Sea View Road now is, with coastguards' cottages built nearby towards the end of this period. Much of the land north of the High Street and east of Roman Bank was "Jungle" – a mixture of trees, sand dunes, marsh and scrubland, with at least one stream running through it.

Tourism began to develop towards the end of the eighteenth century, the first visible sign of which was the building of the Skegness Hotel (later the Vine). Until 1873, this tourism was apparently very genteel and of modest proportions. Everything changed with the arrival of the railway. We have not been able to show, in these notes, what negotiations took place prior to the arrival of the railway. We have, however, been able to illustrate the vision and enterprise of the men and women who were responsible for the development of the town since then, in particular in the last quarter of the nineteenth century and in the two decades after the First World War. By any standards Skegness is well laid out. The maps of Skegness at the turn of the century, which can be viewed in Skegness Library, show an elegant and harmonious design, which was complemented by the development of the Castleton Boulevard area in the 1930's. The development of the Foreshore area from the Waterway in the north to the boating lake and beyond in the south has also stood the test of time.

We have concluded this study in 1939. The war years, which followed immediately and the floods of 1953, were low points in the recent history of Skegness, though, mercifully, Skegness itself suffered less than many of the neighbouring towns and villages from the floods. There have been many developments since the war, some good, some not so good, but the basic structure and "raison d'être" of the town remain. It is still a popular family holiday resort, which attracts large numbers of visitors each year. The challenge for the next generation will be to continue to promote positive developments, without destroying the natural attractions of the resort.

Census of Population figures
for Skegness and Winthorpe

Year	Number of Inhabitants	
	Skegness	**Winthorpe**
1801	134	221
1811	132	174
1821	150	233
1831	185	244
1841	316	273
1851	366	299
1861	322	305
1871	349	285
1881	1338	337
1891	1488	326
1901	2140	379
1911	3775	511
1921	9246	698
1931	9121*	
1951	12539	
1961	12847	
1971	13578	
1981	14629	
1991	16809	
2001	18910	

Source: Census data, plus various secondary sources.

* Winston Kime, in *Skeggy*, notes: "Although the parish of Winthorpe was incorporated with Skegness in 1925, the 1931 census shows a smaller population than in 1921. This is probably accounted for by the dates on which the 1921 and 1931 censuses were taken. In 1921 the count was made on June 19th/20th, when a number of seasonal residents would be included. In 1931 the census was taken two months earlier, on April 26th/27th, when the holiday season had not really begun."

Skegness Parish Register: 1653–1812

Years	Baptisms			Burials			
							of which
	Male	Female	Total	Male	Female	Total	Children
1653–63	10	6	16	11	9	20	8
1664–74	6	5	11	11	8	19	7
1674–84	10	6	16	12	4	16	4
1684–94	13	4	17	7	8	15	2
1694–1712*	10	8	18	11	7	18	4
1712–22	8	14	22	12	15	27	3
1722–31	16	12	28	16	9	25	9
1732–41	19	18	37	10	15	25	15
1742–51	8	11	19	9	12	21	4
1752–61	8	11	19	5	9	14	4
1762–71	12	18	30	11	5	16	4
1772–81	17	14	31	10	11	21	6
1782–91	17	10	27	15	5	20	6
1792–1801	19	18	37	7	10	17	10
1802–12	23	17	40	14	12	26	10
Totals	196	172	368	161	139	300	96

Source: Skegness Parish Register 1653 –1812, Skegness Library BL. SKEGNESS 929.3/1

Notes:

a. The entries for the period 1673 to 1721 begin on Lady Day and end on Lady Day the following year. The other entries are for calendar years.

b. The figures for children are mainly based on entries which say "son of" or "daughter of", but also include, for example, "boy drowned age 9".

c. The figures are for 10 year periods, apart from the first and last rows of figures, which are for 11 year periods.

---

* The records for the period 1700–1708 have been lost.

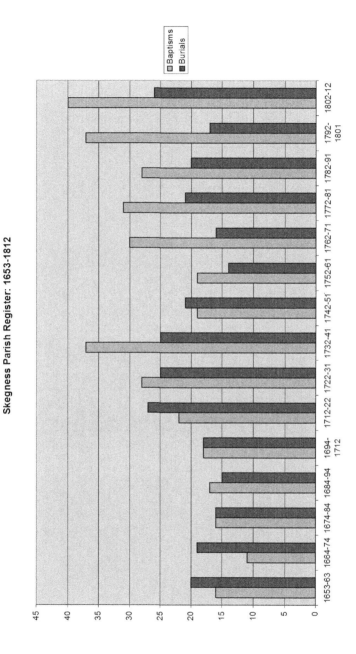

Skegness Parish Register: 1653-1812

Volume 2

SKEGNESS

THROUGH THE YEARS

Skegness in the 17th and 18th Centuries

Skegness: From an agricultural village to a seaside town

Men of Influence:

The Earls of Scarbrough

Mr Henry Vivian Tippet

Mr Rowland Henry Jenkins

Skegness U3A Local History Group

CONTENTS

FOREWORD

In 2005, the Local History Group of the Skegness Branch of the University of the Third Age (U3A) produced a booklet containing notes on the Local History Skegness from the earliest times to 1939. At the suggestion of Ruth Neller in Skegness Library, we then embarked upon a series of individual projects on aspects of Skegness local history. One of our members, Marjorie Wilkinson, has published one of these projects, entitled *Skegness at War*, separately and so we have not reproduced it here.

The present document brings together five remaining projects. There are two articles on the history of Skegness:

Skegness in the Seventeenth and Eighteenth Centuries by James Mackley *and*

Skegness: From an agricultural village to a seaside town by Jennifer Mackley.

There follow three short articles on men who have had a significant influence on the development of Skegness:

The Earls of Scarbrough by Carrol Morris, Kenneth Wilkinson and James Mackley,

Mr Henry Vivian Tippet and his contribution to the development of Skegness by Kenneth Wilkinson and

Mr Rowland Henry Jenkins and his contribution to the development of the Skegness Foreshore, also by Kenneth Wilkinson.

We would like to thank Ruth Neller for her advice at the outset of this project and David Robinson, Richard Gurnham and Winston Kime who gave us valuable guidance and encouragement in the course of our work.

Finally, we would like to thank the staff of Skegness Library for their help with this project.

Skegness, September 2007

SKEGNESS IN THE SEVENTEENTH AND EIGHTEENTH CENTURIES

James Mackley

Introduction

Skegness in the early seventeenth century was a very small farming community of probably fewer than thirty families. The proximity of what was then called "the German Ocean" was of very little consequence to the local economy, except in the constant battle to preserve farming land from the encroaching sea and to make the marshland suitable for grazing.[161] The Earl of Scarbrough's ancestors owned most of the land. The only building that has survived today from the beginning of that century is St. Clement's Church. This had been built in the sixteenth century after the old church had been *"clene consumid and eten up with the se"*.[162] It was in St. Clement's Church that the only significant record relating to the seventeenth and eighteenth centuries was kept. This was the Skegness Parish Register, which began in 1653.

The present study is based on a detailed examination of that Register from its beginning in 1653 to 1812.[163] The aim is to try to

---

[161] Joan Thirsk, *English Peasant Farming* (London: Routledge & Kegan Paul, 1957), records that in the sixteenth and early seventeenth centuries, the parish of Skegness had surrendered to the sea two hamlets, a cony warren and the church (p. 144). These disasters were accompanied by the collapse of the old sea wall in the 1570s and the breaching of an inner seabank, built when the loss of the older one seemed imminent, forty years later. On the other hand she records that an enquiry into land regained from the sea in Wainfleet, Croft and Skegness had established that *"at Skegness where 59 ½ acres had been lost to the sea in 1575, 400 acres had been enclosed in 1618 and another 400 acres since then"* (p. 68).

[162] Quoted by Winston Kime in *Skeggy: the story of an East Coast town* (Skegness, Lincs: Seashell Books, 1969).

[163] *An exact copy of the Skegness Parish Register*, Skegness Library, BL. SKEGNESS 929.3. There is no indication on the document of who undertook this painstaking work. A footnote to the printed version of the Register states:

Parish Registers were unknown until the reign of Henry VIII. In 1538 a Royal Injunction was published by Cromwell, the Vicar General, ordering the clergy to keep Parish Registers, as follows: – "The Curate of every parish church shall keep one book of register, which book he shall every Sunday take forth in the presence of the Churchwardens or one of them write and record in the same all the weddings, christ'nings, and burials, made the whole week before; and for every time that the same shall be omitted shall forfeit to the said church iij s. iiij d. (3/4)". There are 812 Registers now in existence entries in which date back to the year 1588, build up a picture of the people who lived in Skegness during that time.

Population

Over the 151-year period, there were 368 baptisms and 300 burials (*see* Table 1).[164] This suggests a growing population. However, the figures take no account of inward or outward migration. Nor do they take account of the (relatively small) number of people who were buried in Skegness, but obviously did not live there (e.g. "corpses of three sailors and a woman all unknown cast on the shore" in 1811.) Between 1653 and 1721, burials exceeded baptisms, whereas for the next 90 years, there were considerably more baptisms than burials.

Census figures for Skegness are available for only two of the years covered by this study: 1801 and 1811. The population of Skegness was 134 and 132 respectively. The population of England grew rapidly in the second half of the eighteenth century, with the advent of industrialisation. Skegness was a long way away from the new population centres, but it was probably nevertheless a net exporter of population.

All this suggests that in 1650 the population was somewhat lower than in 1801, that it declined slightly over the next 70 years and increased gradually over the next 80 years. It is impossible to put reliable figures on this, but it is safe to assume that at no time between 1653 and 1801 was the population greater than 140, or about 30 families.

---

but those are copies on parchment of the first registers which were in paper, in accordance with the injunctions of 1547 and 1608.

During the civil war, owing to the general confusion and the deposition of the clergy, many registers were lost; but in 1653 after Cromwell had dispersed the Long Parliament the clergy were ordered to give up the keeping of the registers to laymen to be called "Parish Registers." The Skegness Register begins in this year 1653.

[164] The records for the period 1700 to 1708 have been lost.

Table 1

Skegness Parish Register: 1653–1812

Years	Baptisms			Burials			
							of which
	Male	Female	Total	Male	Female	Total	Children
1653–63	10	6	16	11	9	20	8
1664–74	6	5	11	11	8	19	7
1674–84	10	6	16	12	4	16	4
1684–94	13	4	17	7	8	15	2
1694–1712*	10	8	18	11	7	18	4
1712–22	8	14	22	12	15	27	3
1722–31	16	12	28	16	9	25	9
1732–41	19	18	37	10	15	25	15
1742–51	8	11	19	9	12	21	4
1752–61	8	11	19	5	9	14	4
1762–71	12	18	30	11	5	16	4
1772–81	17	14	31	10	11	21	6
1782–91	17	10	27	15	5	20	6
1792–1801	19	18	37	7	10	17	10
1802–12	23	17	40	14	12	26	10
Totals	196	172	368	161	139	300	96

Source: Skegness Parish Register 1653–1812, Skegness Library BL. SKEGNESS 929.3/1

Notes:
a. The entries for the period 1673 to 1721 begin on Lady Day and end on Lady Day the following year. The other entries are for calendar years.
b. The figures for children are mainly based on entries which say "son of" or "daughter of", but also include, for example, "boy drowned age 9".
c. The figures are for 10 year periods, apart from the first and last rows of figures, which are for 11 year periods.

---

* The records for the period 1700–1708 have been lost.

The families

One of the most striking features of the Register is that, over the period, there are a large number of different surnames: 159 surnames, compared with the total number of baptisms and burials (668). 111 surnames appear fewer than 4 times. Thus, there is evidence of a mobile population. There is only one Smith. There are no references to the well-known Skegness names of Grunnill[165] and Perrin, while another old Skegness name, Moody, appears only twice – in 1682 and 1685.

Two-fifths (269 out of 668) of the entries in the Register relate to eleven family names. These are: Bowring (Bowron, Bowrin) (57),[166] Green (46), Chapman (27), Miller (Millar, Millins) (25), Everington (22), Dickinson (Dickison, Dickson) (18), Enderby (18), Walls (18), Grummitt (14), Cotnam (Cotman) (13) and Clarke (Clerke, Clerk, Clark) (11).[167] There are also 12 entries relating to Thompson, but these concern two different families, one of whom was the rector of Skegness.

Table 2 shows how long these eleven families lived in Skegness. The Greens are the only family to appear throughout the whole period of the Register (six generations).

Up to 1720, there were five main families in Skegness: Chapman (gentry), Green, Enderby, Cotnam and Clarke. For a brief period in the 1740s, nine of the eleven main families mentioned in the Skegness Register were living in Skegness. Only the Clarkes had disappeared and the Millers had not yet arrived. By 1756, the Cotnams and Chapmans had disappeared too. From 1786, only four

---

[165] These families probably lived outside the parish of Skegness, for example at Gibraltar Point (in Croft or Wainfleet parishes). Mr Frank Grunnill has confirmed that his family has lived in the Skegness area since at least the middle of the seventeenth century and that some of his ancestors lived at Gibraltar Point.

[166] Original spellings and abbreviations in the Register have been preserved in this document, even when it leads to inconsistencies. Figures in brackets relate to the number of entries in the baptisms and burials register.

[167] Of the 37 *births* recorded, 33 were fathered by four men (*see* Table 3 on page 69); regrettably, many of these children died in infancy.

of the main "Skegness" families remained: named Green, Everington, Enderby and Bowring. In addition, the Millers had arrived. As a publican, William Millar can be seen as the first of a new generation of Skegness residents (though some of his namesakes were shepherds). The Enderby family is first mentioned in 1692 and continues to be found in documents about Skegness after the end of the period of this study. Similarly, though the Everingtons arrived later (first mentioned in 1743) they continued to be important throughout the nineteenth century.

Table 2

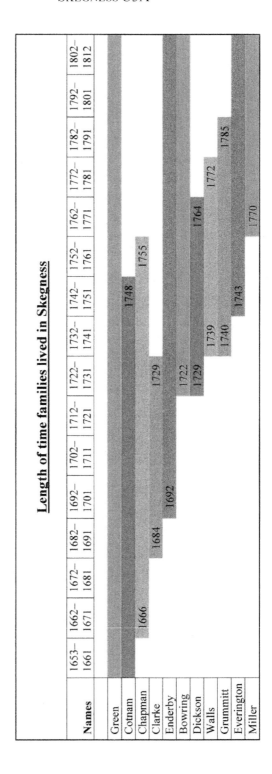

Length of time families lived in Skegness

Christian names

196 males and 172 females were baptised during the period of the Register. Thirty different boys' names were used, the most common being John (used 48 times), William (36), Thomas (30), George (13), Joseph and Robert (10 each). The more unusual names were Hussey and Thory (Chapman) (both the maiden names of their respective mothers), St. John (Bowrin) (married to Lydia Lucy), Adelard, Cornelius, Edmund, Elias, Endbert, Isaac, Lenton, Matthias, Petagrine and Cuthbert. Other names used were Andrew, Charles (5), Edward (5), Henry, James (2), Jeremiah, Matthew (3), Nathaniel (4), Philip, Richard (6) and Samuel (4).

Thirty-three different girls' names are used. The most common are Elizabeth (used 38 times) and Mary (used 37 times), followed by Ann (Anne and Anna) (27) and Susannah (and Susan) (13). The most interesting name was Mary Avice, daughter of St. John and Lydia Lucy. Other less common names were Abigail, Avis (2), Esther (2), Everin, Mildred, Naomi (2), Neeley, Odlin, Thomasina and Zilla. Other names used were Alice, Amy, Bridget, Catharine (2), Charlotte, Dinah (2), Eleanor (2), Eliza (2), Frances (9), Hannah (2), Harriet, Jane (4), Joan, Maria (2), Mabel, Martha, Rebecca (2) and Sarah (9). Mention must also be made here of Endocia Haller, wife of William Haller, shepherd, who bore three sons and a daughter between 1782 and 1785.

It was not at all unusual for the same Christian names to be used by the same parents a second and even a third time after the first one had died: for example, there were two Thory Chapmans baptised in successive years.

The social order

What sort of people lived in Skegness in the eighteenth century? At one end of the social scale, there were "gentlemen" and rectors.

Gentlemen

Plaques in St. Clement's Church describe William and Hussey Chapman as gentlemen. The family lived in Skegness for almost a hundred years at least from 1666 until Ann Chapman's death in 1755. One of the few other people to be referred to as "Mr" in the Register, Mr Burton Rayner, and his wife, Ann, had two daughters in 1766 and 1767. It is possible that the Rayners took over the Chapman residence.

Rectors and curates

There were only six rectors or curates in the 145 years between 1667 and 1812 (and, remarkably, only 3 in the 112 years between 1667 and 1779).

Thomas Thompson was rector of Skegness from 1667 until 1718 – 51 years! He and his wife, Mary, had 6 children between 1674 and 1682. Of these, one died. Mary died in 1684, possibly during her seventh pregnancy.

R. Bursey was rector between 1719 and 1746, while Thomas Garmston was rector from 1747 to 1779. According to the Register, John Johnson was *curate* from 1780 to 1796, followed by E. Greene from 1797 to the end of the register in 1812. However, a board in St. Clement's Church shows Samuel Partridge, Francis Swan and Dr. John Parsons, respectively, as *rectors* from 1780 to 1834. Presumably, the living was insufficient to sustain the lifestyle a university-trained theologian would expect at that time.

This board also shows that George Viscount Castleton, an ancestor of the Earls of Scarbrough, had taken over as patron of the living at the time of the arrival of Thomas Thompson in 1667. The patronage remained in the family until 2004.

William Willson, rector of Skegness from 1938 to 1944, discovered a document dated 25 September 1722 and signed by R. Bursey, Rector, which enumerates the tithes, holdings fees and other emoluments by which the rectors of Skegness were supported at that time:

In primis, the Churchyard consisting of one rood of land or thereabout. Item, all tythes of sheep, viz. wool and lamb in kind throughout the parish. Item, all tythes of feeding and depasturing of cattle. Item, all tythes of pigs, geese, hens, turkeys, ducks, bees, hemp, flax, fruit, garden tythes, thatch and willows. Item, all Easter dues, viz. every communicant 2d., every fire-hearth 1d., every foul [sic] 1d., every calf 2d. Item, all Churchings, Mortuarys, Marriages and Burials.[168]

William Willson also refers to a document which gives "the astonishing information that in 1791 St Clement's actually had a surpliced choir, musically trained":

Paid John Bowring for larning [sic] them to sing ………£1 1s. 0.

Washing surplices: 10s 6d.
Airing 'em:………….1s 6d.
……………………….12s. 0.[169]

Willson goes on to say that in 1812 the organist's salary was increased to two guineas and "in the same year, the Churchwardens in a fit of recklessness spent the sum of 12d on repairs to the organ." He added: "it is greatly to the credit of Skegness that so much care as this was bestowed on decency of public worship at the period in question; for that was an age when, in the Church of England, beauty of Church buildings and furniture, seemliness of ritual and enthusiasm of religious feeling were alike regarded with a mixture of suspicion and contempt."

Tenant farmers and graziers
Many of the main Skegness families – the Greens, the Bowrings, the Everingtons and the Enderbys – are described at some time as

---

[168] Extract from *The Story of Skegness Churches* Revised and enlarged by William F Willson, Rector of Skegness 1938–44, printed on a board in St. Clement's Church.
[169] This was probably John Bowring, who died, aged 49, in 1809.

"graziers". They would probably have been tenant farmers on land owned by the Earl of Scarbrough or his ancestors (the Enderby and Everington families certainly were), though some of them obviously fell on harder times and are sometimes described as "labourer". Representatives of all these families were churchwardens at some time during the period covered by the Register.

Sailors and fishermen
Considering that the modern economy of Skegness is based on its proximity to the sea, during the period under review, the sea appeared to be of little consequence. There are only 13 references to burials related to the sea. In 1717, John Pilmor, Wm. Baines, Tho Hudson and one John, a servant, all seamen drowned by storm, were buried. Richard King, a sailor, was buried in 1741. The Old Sailor (otherwise unnamed) was buried in1759. Robert Gill, a shipwrecked sailor, was buried in 1763. A drowned sailor supposed to be about 15 or 16 years old was buried in 1804. The corpses of three sailors and of a woman all unknown cast on the shore were buried in 1811. Finally, the last entry in the Register records that the corpse of a sailor (unknown) cast on Skegness shore was buried on 22 September 1812.

Of these, only "the Old Sailor" and possibly Richard King could be considered to be residents of Skegness, when they died.

There are only two references to "fishermen" in the Register: one birth and one burial (Thomas Green, a fisherman, buried in 1785, John, son of John Green, fisherman, baptised in 1805).

Publicans
One can almost sense the association of "publicans and sinners" when mention is made of publicans in the Register.[170] Only three references are neutral in tone: the baptism of William Millar's son in 1780, William's burial in 1797 and the baptism of Thomas Melsar's daughter in 1809. John Petty gets a bad press: when she was buried

---

[170] The only hotel in Skegness before 1805 was the Skegness Hotel, now the Vine.

aged 6 years in 1800, Susanna was described as daughter of John Petty, publican, and Susanna, a former wife. In 1804, John "illegitimate son of Mary Houghton (& Jno Petty Publican her master)" was baptised, while Frances "illegitimate daughter of Mary Houghton by John Petty Publican her late master" was baptised in 1806. John Petty was the landlord of the New Inn, later Hildreds.

Labourers

Most of the young family men were farm labourers: of the 40 children baptised between 1800 and 1812, 25 were fathered by labourers. (The other fathers were graziers (8 children) publicans (4) and a shepherd, a fisherman and a sojourning soldier (1 each).

Servants

There are four references to servants being buried in the course of the register, all female. The first was Elizabeth Wilson, who is described as "maid servant of Mr William Chapman" and was buried in 1677. The second was Lidia Medcalfe, also a maidservant, buried in the following year. Two more servants were buried in 1777 and 1807, respectively. This suggests that there were a few better-off families in Skegness, who employed maid-servants, including the Chapmans, the rector, some of the better-off tenant farmers and latterly the hotelkeepers.

Paupers

Skegness obviously had its share of poor people. Between 1741 and 1812, there are at least eight references to "paupers", "poor man" and "poor widow".[171] In some cases this represents a fall from grace. For example, William Lawrence was the son of a churchwarden, but died

---

[171] Ann Jacklin a Poor Widow buried 27.7.1769.
Wm Grummitt a Poor Man buried 10.11.1770.
Wm Lawrence a Poor Man buried 16.11.1770.
Ann Clark a Poor Woman buried 2.6.1774.
Wm Leak a poor Man buried 4.6.1777.
Mary Leak a poor woman buried 1782.
John Nelsey a poor labourer 1789
Thomas Ellis a pauper aged 82 years buried 28.9.1811.

a poor man in 1770. Similarly, Dorcas Green bore a large number of children up to 1748 when her husband died, but she died a poor woman 36 years later.

Illegitimate children

Some of the keepers of the register pull no punches as far as illegitimate children are concerned. Seven are described as "illegitimate" and three as "bastard". John Petty is the only father named. A pointed reference is made too to "widow" Smalley whose daughter, Ann, was baptised in September 1743, two years after the death of John Smally, a pauper, in August 1741. There appears to have been some inconsistency, however, in the treatment of illegitimacy in the register (or rectors may have refused to baptise illegitimate children) because all but one of the entries relate to the periods 1761 to 1778 and 1804 to 1808. These periods are all contained within the periods when Thomas Garmston was rector (1747 to 1779) or E. Greene was curate (1797 to the end of the register in 1812).[172]

Health and longevity

Size of families

Of the eleven main families referred to in Table 2, all have at least one father with four or more children. Many of these died, as the following table (Table 3) shows.

---

[172] Abigail Bastard Daughter of Alice Waterman baptised 17.4.1685.
Eliz: the Illegitimate Daughter of Mary Hall baptised 24.5.1761.
Mabel the Illegitimate Daughter of Susanna Almonds baptised 10.1.1762.
Dinah the Bastard Daughter of Ann Graham baptised 17.8.1767.
Susannah the Illegitimate of Ann Twigg baptised 26.10.1772.
Ann the Bastard Daughter of Mary Woods baptised 8.2.1778.
John illegitimate son of Mary Houghton (& Jno Petty Publican her master) baptised 23.12.1804.
Frances illegitimate daughter of Mary Houghton (by John Petty Publican her late master) baptd 2.3.1806.
John illegitimate son of Catherine Dower baptised 16.6.1805.
Isaac illegitimate son of Mildred Ostler baptised 11.12.1808.

Table 3

Large families

Family	Children of one father	Number of these who died
Green (1)	9	3
Green (2)	8	2
Cotnam	4	0
Chapman (1)	12	1
Chapman (2)	10	2
Clarke	4	0
Enderby	6	0
Bowring (1)	9	7
Bowring (2)	10	3
Bowring (3)	7	1
Bowring (4)	7	1
Dickinson	6	4
Walls	10	2
Grummitt	8	1
Everington	8	3
Miller	8	1

Infant and child mortality

In England as a whole in 1700, "maybe a fifth of all babies died in their first year; perhaps one in three died – of gastro-enteric disorders and fevers – before the age of five."[173] These figures are mirrored closely in Skegness during the 150-year period. Ninety-six (almost one third) of the 300 burials during the period were children. Surprisingly, the figures were lower for the period up to 1731, when "only" 23% of burials were children. The 1730s were a bad period for child mortality with 15 out of the 22 burials being children (spread throughout the decade). The last twenty-one years (from 1792 to 1812) also saw a large proportion of child burials with 20 out of the 43 burials during this period being children.

---

[173] Roy Porter, *English Society in the Eighteenth Century* (London: Penguin, 1983), p. 13.

Disease

In England as a whole, 1718–19, 1727–31 and 1740–42 were particularly bad years for typhus, typhoid and other fevers.[174] The figures involved for Skegness are too small to draw firm conclusions. However, it is possibly noteworthy that in none of these 7 years did baptisms exceed burials, while burials exceeded baptisms in all but two of them. By contrast, in the 9 years 1731 to 1739 (inclusive), burials never exceeded baptisms and baptisms exceeded burials in all but two of those years.

Longevity

At least one early commentator recorded that Skegness was not a particularly healthy place in the eighteenth century, because of the prevalence of marsh fever.[175] Dutton, on the other hand, says evidence from gravestones suggests Skegness was a healthy place. "In looking over the tombstones the visitor [to St. Clement's Church] will notice that most of the ages are more than the allotted span, which speaks well of Skegness as a health resort."[176]

There is, in fact, not much evidence one way or the other from the Register. We have, however, been able to work out the approximate ages of 13 men who died in Skegness between 1708 and 1812.[177] The three oldest were William Chapman, gentleman, aged 82, his son, Hussey, aged 73, and Thomas Ellis, a pauper, aged 82. The ages of the others ranged from 38 (John Enderby 1774) to 59 (Thomas Green, 1785, though this person could have been a younger man of the same name). The *mean* average age of these thirteen men was 59. The *median* age was 52.

---

[174] Porter, *op.cit.* p. 202.
[175] Edmund Oldfield, *A Topographical and Historical Account of Wainfleet and the Wapentake of Candleshoe, in the County of Lincoln* (London: Longman, Rees et al, 1829).
[176] Geo. H.J. Dutton, *Ancient & Modern Skegness,* 1922, p. 75.
[177] From entries in the Register, plaques in St. Clement's Church and a booklet on Church Farm Museum (Church Farm Museum, *A Place with a Past*, Lincolnshire County Council, p. 45.)

All but one of the five women whose ages are recorded between 1798 and 1812 (excluding one who died after childbirth) were between 72 and 80. The other woman was 52 when she died.

From this limited evidence, one can draw the conclusion that most men did not live much beyond 50. Women lived longer, provided they survived childbirth, but many women died within two years after the birth of a child, presumably during or soon after childbirth or a further pregnancy.

Housing

At any one time, there were probably not more than 30 families with different names living in Skegness.

Where did these people live? The only building that was standing at the beginning of this period, which is still standing, is St Clement's Church. That was said to have been built in the fields, way back from the sea. John Enderby is first recorded as farming the Church Farm, which is nearby, in 1766. The Skegness Hotel, later the Vine, was advertised in *The Stamford Mercury* in 1772 as "standing on as clean a shore as any in England". A sketch map of 1793 (*see* Map 1) shows a total of 8 houses in the "central" area of Skegness (including the junction of Wainfleet Road and Roman Bank, the current High Street and the beginning of what is now Drummond Road).[178] There would also have been other houses outside the area covered by the map. So, at the end of the eighteenth century, the Enderbys lived at Church Farm, while it is possible that some of the Dickinsons and/or Millers lived at the Skegness Hotel. The rector, if resident, would have lived at the rectory, which, if it existed, would have stood near to St. Clement's Church, while there was also, presumably, a house of some standing formerly occupied by the Chapmans. McKinley House (the Moat House) was built

---

[178] Skegness, 1793, based on a rough map referring to the Massingberd-Mundy lands.

around 1780 and was inhabited in 1793 by the Revd E. Walls.[179] The Everington and Bowring families lived in farm houses or cottages (the Bowring house is shown on the map of 1793, as is Everington's land). Six or seven other families of graziers may have also lived in similar properties.

Most of the remaining 10 or 20 households probably lived in very poor accommodation: some were single mothers, while others are described as poor or paupers. So, there would have been a maximum of 35 housing units (30 is a more probable upper limit) in Skegness during this period, of which only two: the Vine and Church Farm, still exist.

In England generally, housing conditions (other than for the wealthy) were poor: the rural poor inhabited "shacks made of wattle, turf and road-scrapings".[180] Indeed, it was recorded that in order to discourage poor-law settlements many parishes demolished cottages and refused permission to build new ones.[181] It is not surprising, therefore, that none of these dwellings have survived. There is, however, an example of a 'mud and stud' cottage built in this period at Church Farm Museum. This would have been the most likely form of housing for most of the inhabitants of Skegness.

Roads

The sketch map of Skegness in 1793 referred to in the previous section shows a "Publick High Road", a road to Winthorpe and Burgh (Roman Bank), a road to Croft and Wainfleet, and a "Publick Road [formerly High Road to Gibraltar Point now impassable]". Interestingly, there is reference to Revd Mr Walls' old house which had been washed away by the sea (clearly within living memory at that time). The roads at the time would, of course have been little more than cart tracks, some of which would have been covered in

---

[179] This is not the same Walls as the family referred to in this study.

[180] Porter, *op. cit.* p. 215.

[181] Porter, *op. cit.* p. 215.

stone. Roads in England in 1700 were described as "perhaps worse than the Romans had left them".[182] Though the standard of roads improved in England generally in the eighteenth century, it is doubtful whether these improvements reached Skegness. Even by 1849 a map covering a wider area (*see* Map 2) showed little change in the layout of Skegness. This shows *only* High Street, Wainfleet Road, Burgh Road, Roman Bank and Sea View Lane, all of which probably existed in 1793, but does not show Drummond Road.[183]

Conclusion

Skegness in the seventeenth and eighteenth centuries was a very small settlement of no more than 30 dwellings. In previous centuries it may have had a castle, a harbour and a ferry crossing to Norfolk.[184] But by 1650 these had long since gone. The small church had been rebuilt in the fields about a mile from the sea. The area bordering the sea was a mixture of sand dunes and marshes. This marshland was constantly being eroded and reclaimed for grazing.

A core of eleven families accounts for two-fifths of the 668 baptisms and burials recorded in the Skegness Parish Register between 1653 and 1812. These include the Chapmans, gentry, whose memory is recorded on plaques in St. Clement's Church; the Bowrings and the Everingtons whose names are mentioned on an eighteenth century map (both tenant farmers); and the Enderbys who were the tenants of Church Farm. The Greens were the only family to survive the whole 150-year period of the Register. The rest of the population was fairly mobile with 159 different surnames recorded, including 111 which appear fewer than 4 times. For such a small parish, the rectors stayed a long time: only 3 between 1667 and 1779.

---

[182] Porter, *op. cit.* p. 11.

[183] Winston Kime, *The Book of Skegness: Ingoldmells, Addlethorpe and Chapel St. Leonards* (Buckingham: Barracuda, 1986), based on a map of S. Hill & Son, Croft, 1849.

[184] Arthur Owen and Richard Coates, 'Traiectus/Tric/Skegness: A Domesday Name Explained,' *Lincolnshire History and Archaeology*, No 38, 2003.

The most popular Christian names of baptised babies were John, William and Thomas for boys and Elizabeth, Mary and Ann (with variations) for girls.

Farming was the predominant occupation of the men of Skegness. Much of the land was owned by the Earls of Scarbrough, though it was farmed by tenant farmers. There may have been independent small holders, but there is no evidence of this. Sea-based activities were peripheral to the economy of the village: only two men are recorded in the Parish Register as fishermen.

Infant mortality was high. As in the rest of England at the time, almost a third of the burials recorded relate to children. Not many of the ages of the adults buried are recorded, but the overall picture, with exceptions, is that most men did not live much beyond 50. Women lived longer (into their seventies), provided that they survived the child-bearing period, but many of them did not.

Only two buildings survive from this period: St. Clement's Church and the Vine Hotel. Neither was in the centre of Skegness – the area around High Street, Wainfleet Road and Roman Bank. Much of the population would have lived in mud and stud cottages near farms away from the centre of the village.

The first signs of change appeared towards the end of the eighteenth century, with the building of the Skegness Hotel (now The Vine). From then on Skegness gradually, and very slowly, would begin to develop into the tourist attraction that it has become today. But at the end of the period of this study, the event which would change the face of Skegness for ever – the arrival of the railway in 1873 – was a long way off. The population of Skegness in 1811 was 132 – probably only slightly greater than it had been in 1653.

SKEGNESS:
FROM AN AGRICULTURAL
VILLAGE
TO A SEASIDE TOWN

Jennifer Mackley

Contents

Chapter One

Skegness – the village

Skegness was a sleepy backwater for most of the time before the early part of the nineteenth century. It is true that in Roman times roads reached the shoreline in several places. Burgh le Marsh is known to have been a Roman town with a shore fort near Skegness. There was probably a ferry from there across to Thornham, near Brancaster, in Norfolk. Moreover, there were signs of a flourishing town in the early sixteenth century, but the 'ness' or nose of Skegness (a ridge of sand dunes which formed a promontory south-south-east from near Ingoldmells) gave way and, by 1526, the old town of Skegness began to be submerged by the incoming sea. When Leyland visited that part of the country in 1540, the *"sumtyme great haven town"* which traded in Baltic timber had completely disappeared.

In 1568, the Commissioners of Sewers arranged for the building of a new bank to act as a sea defence. The Roman Bank north of Lumley Square in Skegness became this new sea defence. It was completed in 1574. One hundred years later in 1670 Lord Castleton enclosed the outer marshes with a Green Bank between the High Street and North Shore Road, leaving the muddy foreshore outside the enclosure. This eventually became the sand dunes of the 'jungle'. The land remained in the hands of the Saunderstons for another fifty years, but when the 5th Viscount and only Earl of Castleton died without an heir in 1723, he left his entire fortune to Thomas Lumley, the son of his cousin the 1st Earl of Scarbrough. In 1856 Richard George succeeded to the title and became 9th Earl of Scarborough. He is widely seen as being the 'father' of modern day Skegness.

During the early seventeenth century, wool production was the basis of the rural economy. The Lincolnshire marshland, as distinct from the Fens, made great sheep and cattle pasture. It consisted of a large green fertile plain between the Wolds and the sea, about

45 miles long and between 5–10 miles wide from Wainfleet to the Humber. In 1636, the grazing area around Skegness supported 1200 sheep and a large number of cattle and horses. There were very few trees in and around Skegness. What wood there was came from shipwrecks or from the Wolds, consequently the houses of the time were built of mud and stud.

During the eighteenth century, coal was landed at Skegness, but not in particularly large quantities. Burrell Massingberd imported coal in his own ships around 1726. Most of his ships docked in Boston, but some supplies he sent up the coast to Skegness for his own use at Gunby Hall and for the use of his tenants and neighbours. During the early part of the nineteenth century, about 6,000 tons of coal a year were brought in by sea from Wallsend on the Tyne. Billy boys discharged their cargo straight onto the shore and the coal was then carted from there via the Sea View Pullover to a coal yard on Burgh Road or to the coal yard that existed where Tower Gardens is today. Shingle also arrived by sea to supplement that which was dug from pits along what is now Drummond Road. This was used to form the hardcore for some of the roads across the Marshes.

The eighteenth and early nineteenth centuries were also the heyday for smuggling and contraband trading along the Lincolnshire coastline. The most successful smuggling was accomplished on the open sandy shores between the custom stations of Saltfleet and Skegness. Here the shore was backed with sand dunes with gaps where carts could be pulled to and from the beach. These gaps were known as 'pullovers'. Along this stretch the locals were skilled in avoiding detection. The old inns were often the meeting place for sailors and others whose activities were not strictly within the law. The Vine is amongst the oldest secular buildings in Skegness and in 1902, a skeleton with brass buttons was found in the walls. It is believed to be a Customs Officer who had disappeared years earlier.

Chapter Two

The 'new cult of sea bathing'

The cult of sea bathing came relatively late to the Lincolnshire coast, partly because of the remoteness of the coast and the lack of decent roads. In earlier times, the area around Skegness was not considered to be healthy. The inhabitants were subject to ague and fevers produced by the effluvia, generally termed 'marsh masmata'. It was thought that this came from the stagnant water in the marshes and fens. The enclosure, which took place almost unobtrusively around Skegness at the beginning of the seventeenth century, caused the minimum of distress, but the subsequent drainage of the fens and marshes did much to improve the general health of the inhabitants.

Freiston Shore, *'the Brighton of the middle classes in Lincolnshire'* was the principal Lincolnshire bathing place in 1786. Initially it consisted of *'two inns behind a clay wall looking out over an expanse of sand and samphire towards the Wash'*. Sea bathing was reputed to be good for *'all scorbutic complaints, sore legs, sore eyes, surfeits, hard drinking, nervous habits, hydrophobia and poor appetite'*. Freiston Shore was popular because it was situated only a few miles from Boston and therefore fairly easy to get to. As with Brighton, people went there to see and be seen. Sea bathing at Freiston Shore lasted something over the century, but then it dwindled as the coast silted up and access to other parts of the Lincolnshire coastline became easier.

By the beginning of the nineteenth century Skegness too was feeling the benefit of the current preoccupation with the healthy aspects of sea bathing. As early as 1784, the Vine was advertising in the *London General Evening News*. However, even as late as 1826, Skegness still did not merit an entry of its own in White's Directory. There were only a few paragraphs at the end of the entry for Wainfleet, including the fact that *'Skegness, until lately an obscure village, is rising in celebrity both as a bathing place and as a port. It has several private lodging houses and two large and commodious hotels which are provided with warm and cold shower baths and can each make up 30 beds.'* By 1851, the village still had only 366 inhabitants, a few earning their living as fishermen and the rest employed on farms, or working in the new hotels. Some of the wealthier families from in and around Lincolnshire now came to Skegness in the summer months. From the latter part of the previous century, there had been a stagecoach that ran three times a week from Spilsby to Boston, then on to Spalding and Peterborough. Later a diligence ran on Sunday and Thursday from Boston to Wainfleet and Skegness. During the bathing season, this ran everyday, or a horse and cart could be hired from some of the not too distant villages. By the middle of the century the Peterborough to Grimsby railway line was in use. The train passed about a mile west of Burgh le Marsh and the Skegness hotels sent a horse drawn bus to bring the guests the six or seven miles from the station to the hotels.

The Skegness Hotel was built in 1770. It was renamed first as Enderby's Hotel in 1828 and later in 1851 it became known as the Vine. It was the first hotel to be built to attract visitors who were interested in the new cult of sea bathing. Joseph Dickinson was the landlord in 1772. It was noted that bathing machines were there in 1784, but when the Hon. John Byng arrived in the summer of 1791, he found it *'a vile and shabby place'* with *'no garden, no walk, no billiard room, nor anything for comfort or temptation.'* Things slowly began to improve and ten years later, with George Pigot in charge, the hotel could boast of 20 bedrooms, a garden and a bowling green. Furthermore by 1805 John Stafford had installed *'improved conveniences for heating sea water for bathing.'* By 1806 the Skegness Hotel was clearly popular with the gentry as *'Lady Ingleby Amcott presides and with a condescending attention promotes the conviviality and entertainment of the company.'* Also *'The Dowager Countess of Rothes and the family from Gunby Park dined the other day and the following day a great influx of visitors from Spilsby and the neighbouring town ... augmented the party at dinner to upwards of sixty,'* reported the newspaper. Later, in 1816, John Stafford made the bridle road from

82

Croft Bank to the Skegness Hotel into a *'commodious carriage road'* allowing better access for his upper class visitors.

By this time there was a rival establishment to the Skegness Hotel in the New Hotel. This, it is said, was originally built by the Rev. Edward Walls as a hostel for his friends, but John Petty took it over and in 1805 acquired a new bathing machine for the hotel. Thomas Melson added a second in 1809. He also added a *'most commodious warm sea bath'* and a shower bath in 1818. Ten years later Joseph Hildred took over the hotel. He advertised the hotel in the *Mercury* and was known to have placed the following advertisement on 21st June 1844. *'This Hotel is very pleasantly situated on the Eastern Coast and commands very extensive views of the German Ocean. Vessels of all descriptions from London and the North are constantly passing and repassing in sight'.* When he died in 1848, his widow, Sarah, took over the running of the hotel. It was she who added a billiard room upstairs in 1850 and enlarged the hotel in 1855. Her son Charles took over in 1874, by which time the New Hotel had acquired the family name and was known as Hildred's Hotel.

However, at the beginning of the nineteenth century the Lincolnshire seaside was still only for the relatively well off. Apart from the two hotels in Skegness, there were possibly some 23 houses that could have taken in lodgers, but the population of this small village was still only 134, which was less than the neighbouring Wainfleet All Saints with its population of 506 and Wainfleet St. Mary's, population 421. It was described, in 1827, by an anonymous writer as being *'a retired situation, well adopted for the resort of invalids. It has not usually so much company as Freiston Shore because it is much further from Boston, but for a place where ease and quiet and comfort may be obtained at a reasonable expense, few places can compare with Skegness'.*

The poet Tennyson, who was born in Somersby in 1809, was a frequent visitor to Skegness. As a child, he and his parents travelled in a *'booby-hutch'*, a covered cart, with the family of the Rev. Drummond Rawnsley (of Halton Holegate, near Spilsby) and stayed at the Moat House. Edward Walls built this one room thick house in

1780 for his sister, but later it was let to visitors. It stood just behind the Green Bank (now Drummond Road) and faced the open shore. There was a removable plank bridge from the front door to the Bank. This meant that the young Tennyson could run straight out onto the sandy bank, across the beautiful hard sands, through the salt-water creeks and so to the sea. In later years Tennyson stayed at Enderby's Hotel where he could be seen *'a raavin and taavin upon the sand hills in his shirt sleeves an' all composing poetry aloud'.*

In 1845 Henry Winn, parish clerk, poet, shopkeeper and a self-educated man of considerable talent who lived in Fullesby, visited his brother in Halton Holegate after a period of sickness. He wrote in his diary of 9th September 1845:

> *Hired a horse and cart [at Halton Holegate] this morning and accompanied by my brother, Richard, and sister, Harriet, proceeded to Skegness, a pleasant village on the seacoast. This day was the Annual Life Boat Regatta and meeting of the Wainfleet branch of the shipwrecked fishermen and mariners' society instituted in 1839. The day was a splendid occasion, and considering the time of the harvest, it was really astonishing to see the concourse of people assembled at the village and the number of carriages of almost every description exceeded all I have seen before.*

In spite of the fact that Skegness was gaining a reputation as a bathing resort, the villagers were still mostly employed on the land. Kelly's Post Office Directory of 1849 listed only thirteen professional and trades people in Skegness in that year. The village, itself, consisted of four roads: High Street, Wainfleet Road, Roman Bank and Burgh Road, with a scattering of dwellings mainly connected to the farms. The New Hotel is marked on a map of 1849 (*see* Maps 2 and 3) with a collection of cottages along the western half of the street. The Vine Hotel appears to be situated in the middle of nowhere. Drummond Road is only a sandy track. The Old Ship Inn, originally built in 1830, was on the opposite side of Roman Bank to the present building erected in the 1930s and fields surround St. Clement's Church.

Chapter Three

The Coming of the Railway

Not everyone was in favour of the success the railway was having in England. In 1829, the Duke of Wellington said that he was against the railways because *"it would encourage the lower orders to move about."* He was right. The railway continued to expand throughout the country, allowing more and more of the lower classes to travel further afield.

The Manchester, Sheffield and Lincolnshire Railway, terminating in Grimsby, and the East Lincolnshire Railway (Boston to Grimsby) opened in 1848. From that moment, the nature of the village of Skegness changed. This railway had a station at Burgh le Marsh. The hotel proprietors of Skegness were quick to point out that their part of the Lincolnshire coast was now within easy reach of Burgh station. Each sent an omnibus to meet the trains. The fare was one shilling. The gentle influx of well-to-do visitors was gradually being replaced by people from the industrial towns of the East Midlands, Yorkshire and London. Certainly, during the summer months the visitors could outnumber the residents many times over. In 1861, 3,000 people attended the races in Skegness, practically ten times the resident population. In 1871, a single-track branch line was laid between Firsby and Wainfleet. Atkin's omnibus met the trains and took the passengers to Skegness. The single fare was one shilling, the return fare 1/6d (7.5p)

Two years later, the single track was extended a further five miles to terminate at Skegness. The visitors could now come all the way to the seaside village and come they did in huge numbers. The extension to Skegness was opened on 28th July 1873 just in time to take advantage of the statutory August Bank Holiday (the first Monday in August). All workers were entitled to a holiday on that day thanks to Lubbock's Act of 1871. During the season, thousands of excursionists from the manufacturing districts came to enjoy the sea air and, much to the annoyance of some of the villagers, the railway company started running trains for day trips on Sundays. The single track was not doubled until 1900, so trains coming in and out of Skegness were using the same track. This meant that often the return journeys could run well into the night, with the last train sometimes leaving as late as 2:30 the following morning.

Cheap Day Excursions were run from Nottingham, via Grantham, departing at 7:40 am. Half-Day Specials were offered from Boston. The Bank Holiday Gala of 1874 saw the arrival of 10,000 trippers when the population of Skegness was still only just over 500. In May 1875, a charter train from Kirkstead took 220 people to Skegness to enjoy the *'boating, bathing and other amusements',* followed by a knife and fork supper at the Sea View Hotel. In 1876 the Great Northern Railway advertised a range of Cheap Day Specials to the Skegness races held on the sands in front of the Sea View Hotel. These Cheap Day Specials attracted between 10,000 and 12,000 day trippers. The Day Excursions increased rapidly with no less than 220,000 excursionists coming to Skegness in 1878. By 1881, 25,000 people attended the races and although the resident population of Skegness was now on its way to 1,500, it was still completely unprepared for the influx of visitors who came the following year. In July and August 1882, the excursionists were descending on Skegness at a rate of between 10,000 and 12,000 a week, culminating in a staggering 20,000 on August Bank Holiday Monday.

The middle of the 1880s saw a marked decline in the number of excursionists arriving in Skegness, mainly due to the depression affecting the industrial catchment areas. Even so in 1890 Skegness was described as *'the noisiest and most crowded of the Lincolnshire sea-side places, except Cleethorpes, invaded every day during the summer by an enormous number of excursionists from the Midland counties',* but *'after 6pm the place is again nearly emptied'.* However, by the beginning of the twentieth century the visitors to Skegness began steadily increasing again from 226,887 in 1902; to 321,260 in 1907; 356,409 in 1910 until by 1913 the total number of passengers exceeded three quarters of a million for the first time. The following year in the eight weeks up to the beginning of August 1914, the figure rose to 407,000, but once England was at war the German Ocean no longer held the same appeal. The vast number of trains that had been available to bring excursionists to the seaside were needed to transport the newly recruited soldiers. Moreover, those of the population not actually fighting in the war had other constraints on their time. The heyday of the railway, as far as Skegness was concerned, was over, at least for the foreseeable future.

Chapter Four

Skegness – the town

It was in the late 1870s that the 9th Earl of Scarbrough decided to transform his small coastal village into a lively seaside resort. The boom in farming that had occurred during the French war began to decline with the defeat of the French at Waterloo in 1815. This decline had little effect on the small population of Skegness, which increased from 132 in 1811 to 366 in 1851. There was less demand for agricultural labour, but for the local inhabitants there was the beginning of a small tourist industry and some jobs could be found in the new hotels. However, the decline in agriculture meant that the Earl had to find other ways to safeguard his wealth. He was quick to realise the potential of Skegness as a seaside resort and he, along with his agent Tippet, decided that a 'Grand Plan' (*see* Map 4) was needed to prevent the village from growing haphazardly. He employed the services of Gilbert Dashper, a solicitor, and a Lincolnshire architect by the name of John Whitton, to draw up a plan for the creation of a new seaside town.

He was not the first man to think about transforming a coastal village. The pattern of one-man resort development had begun almost fifty years earlier. New Brighton, Fleetwood and Herne Bay had been founded in the 1830s; Llandudno in the late 1840s and Saltburn in the 1860s. Not all of these had been successful. Llandudno's growth was long delayed and New Brighton hardly grew at all, but the Earl and Tippet knew that if they could get the railway to Skegness, then Skegness could be transformed into a thriving community.

The Earl had a vision for his new town. He wanted watering places, wide streets, attractive parades and other amenities. He wanted new hotels, boarding houses, pleasure gardens, esplanades and a pier. When the railway arrived in 1873, Tippet had already had the valuer J.H. Vessey inspect the foreshore of Skegness with *'a view of offering the land for the erection of villas'.* The new town was planned going north from the main village street thus allowing the farmers to keep the better grazing ground to the south and west. The new houses were to be built between Roman Bank and the sea and as the development spread, tenant farmers were forced to leave the land. Although the 'Grand Plan' was not drawn up until 1878, many acres of farmland north of the old village street had been taken from the tenants (chiefly William Everington). Where the Earl's jurisdiction could not be questioned there was little difficulty in evicting tenants, but some of the tenants living on Roman Bank came under the jurisdiction of the Commissioners of Sewers and to obtain their eviction the solicitors Tweed & Stephen were heavily involved. However, very little was paid out in compensation. By 1879, the amount of compensation was only just over £500.

Plans were exhibited at railway stations in Nottingham, Derby, Leicester, Boston, Lincoln, Grantham, Peterborough, Grimsby, Sheffield, Leeds, Bradford, Doncaster and at King's Cross. They showed that 787 houses were to be built in the new town. Along with the houses, there was the need for a proper infrastructure. All this activity required skilled workmen. Although some of the villagers could act as labourers, there was a serious shortage of the skilled workers needed for this transformation of Skegness. There was also, in the beginning, a serious shortage of accommodation for those workers coming from the industrial heartland. Some could travel daily from Wainfleet, Burgh or Winthorpe but others had to come from other parts of Lincolnshire or from the East Midland towns now connected by the railway. These workers would certainly need to lodge locally.

We have seen already that in Kelly's Post Office Directory of 1849 only thirteen professional and trades people were listed in Skegness (out of a population of approximately 350). Seven of these were farmers, with Mrs Elizabeth Everington also being listed as a Coal Dealer. The other professional and trades people consisted of the School Master, a Shopkeeper, a Blacksmith, a Boot maker and the two landlords of the Vine and the New Hotel. By 1872, the year before the railway came directly to Skegness, the population statistics were very similar to those of 1849, but the nature of the village was already changing. There were still seven farmers listed, but now several tradesmen lived in Skegness, including a Boat maker, a Bricklayer, a Carpenter and a Joiner. There were also more people catering for the holidaymakers. Samuel and William Tuckworth were Bathing Machine Proprietors and V.C. Crow was the Omnibus Carrier. Skegness could now boast of three shopkeepers and ten people were listed as either a Boarding House keeper or a Lodging House keeper. Mrs Almond had become the Post Mistress. A Coast Guard Officer, a Justice of the Peace, a Parish Clerk, a Sexton, a Curate and the Vicar of Friskney completed the list.

By 1881, eight years after the railway arrived at Skegness, the population had risen to a staggering 1332, almost 1,000 more people than ten years earlier. It was during these years that the Earl of Scarbrough began the transformation of his small agricultural village. He had a vast building project in hand and the coming of the railway meant that workers could come from further afield to take up employment. There were jobs in the building industry, the services for the new town and in the newly built shops, lodging houses, hotels and other amenities needed for the day-trippers and holiday visitors. In 1871, 59% of the inhabitants of Skegness were born either in the village itself or within a five-mile radius. By 1881, Skegness had the power to attract almost 1,000 people from outside that five-mile radius.

In January of 1882, Tippet could tell Mr Cockshott of the Great Northern that

Skegness is steadily and satisfactorily advancing: there are more buildings now in progress than at any time since we started; and of a better class. There is not a house to be let in the place; the amusements and attractions for the visitors are increasing every year, and there is now accommodation for an unlimited number of people. We only want them down and they will readily come if the facilities are offered to them to do so.

The houses and shops stretched almost the length of Lumley Road and boarding houses were beginning to appear along the Parades and on Drummond Road, Rutland Road and Algitha Road.

In December of the same year one of the five freehold land societies owning land in Skegness began laying out a new road (now known as Grosvenor Road) by laying the drainage pipes before being in a position to offer the building plots for sale.

The boom continued until 1883, (just 10 years after the arrival of the railway) but this was the peak. In May 1884, The *Herald* stated that *'not many new buildings have been erected in Skegness during the past winter'* the only record being of 10 cottages completed by Mr Joseph Crawshaw in the new road off Wainfleet Road. By 1886, the situation was much worse, for by then Skegness was suffering the effects of the general depression. Some idea of the extent of this is given by the figures of the number of excursionists carried by the Great Northern Railway to Skegness from 1881–1885. The figures below were printed in the *Skegness Herald*.

April – September	1881	195,671
	1882	230,277
	1883	213,299
	1884	224,225
	1885	118,473

The population figures for Skegness taken from the census of 1881 and 1891 show nothing of the extent the effects of the depression might have had on the town's people. In fact, the census reports a slight increase from 1332 in 1881 to 1488 in 1891. However, it is possible that these figures could hide a significant fall in the population, probably after 1883 but before the returns for 1891. It is known that the builder, T.S. Kassel, who built Rutland Terrace, could only sell the end part (what is today the Masonic Hall) and therefore was forced into bankruptcy. Other builders could well have suffered the same fate, causing hardship to their suppliers. This, coupled with a decline in the number of visitors, could have affected the livelihood of many others in the town.

Chapter Five

Amenities for the benefit of the inhabitants of Skegness

The Earl of Scarbrough in his 'Grand Plan' did not just concern himself with accommodation for the residents and the holidaymakers, there was also a vast infrastructure that needed to be organised, if the town was to progress satisfactorily. As mentioned earlier, the huge building project needed many craftsmen and labourers. These people, as well as those who had come to open businesses, had to know that if they brought their families to settle in Skegness, then, as well as adequate housing, there would be churches, schools, clean drinking water and a system in place to deal with law and order.

The main ingredients needed to ensure that this enormous building project continued without interruption was a constant supply of money and a constant supply of bricks. Originally, the Earl of Scarbrough leased the brickworks from James Warth, a local farmer, but he soon found it was impossible to meet the demand for bricks, so in 1882 he bought the Warth and Dunkley brickworks on the Wainfleet Road. By April 1883 new sheds, offices and kilns had been built and two new machines were installed, one of which was capable of producing 1,000 bricks an hour. John Carter opened a second brickworks situated on the Burgh Road in 1882, thus making sure that there would be an ample supply of bricks. There were 170 houses built by 1877 with approximately 200 more added in the five years between 1877 and 1882.

The Gas Company was formed in 1877 and, in 1882, the gasworks were erected on Alexandra Road, near to the railway, at a cost of £3,500. Mr Foster was the manager. The waterworks were constructed in 1879. This belonged to the Earl of Scarbrough, but was managed by Mr Philips and was supplied from an artesian well on the Burgh Road, about half a mile from the town. The water was described as of the *purest and best quality*. A massive 60ft. tower was erected at the works, on top of which was a storage tank capable of holding 10,000 gallons. The water was forced into the tank by a powerful steam pump. Both the gasworks and the waterworks were extended in the 1920s. Also in 1879 a Sewage Farm and works was begun at Cow Bank (now a nature reserve). The scheme, devised by the Durham engineer, D. Balfour, was for land treatment rather than a discharge into the sea, thus making sure that the beaches were kept clean. The Earl of Scarbrough gave £5000 towards the cost. The sanitary authority paid the remaining £1,700. However, it was 1882 before it became fully operational.

St Matthew's Church was the central point of the Earl's original plan. He donated the site in the middle of his wide central boulevard and gave £3,000 towards the building costs. The foundation stone was laid in 1879 and the church, built of stone in the Early English Style according to the design of James Fowler of Louth, was opened in 1880. The old village church of St Clement's, built in the sixteenth century, was seen by the Earl as too small for the increasing population of his new town. The Reverend Francis Baldwin was the first rector at the new church. He came from the vicarage of the Earl of Scarbrough at Maltby in Yorkshire. A Primitive Methodist Chapel had been built on Roman Bank in 1836 when the population of the village was no more than two hundred. A larger chapel, probably made out of wood, was built in 1848 near to where the railway station was eventually situated, only to be replaced by another chapel on Roman Bank in 1899. In 1837 the Wesleyan Chapel was erected in the High Street. This too was replaced by a larger building, situated on Algitha Road, in 1882. The Wesleyan Manse was built in Lumley Road in 1899.

Other religious denominations wanted to bring their particular religious beliefs to the growing population of the town. An inaugural meeting of the Skegness Baptist Church was held in 1894 in the *'tin tabernacle'* in Beresford Avenue. This had originally been used as St Paul's Free Church of England. It had been the home of a breakaway group of Anglicans led by H.V. Tippet. In 1888, this group left St. Matthew's Church, accusing the Rev. Baldwin of *'popish practices'*. However, six or seven years later the group rejoined St. Matthew's Church when the new rector was installed. The local Baptists took over the *'tin tabernacle'*, which was eventually replaced in 1911 by a new brick building. This new church kept the name of St. Paul and became known as St. Paul's Baptist Church. The first Roman Catholic Church, Sacred Heart, was opened in 1898 in Grosvenor Road. It had cost £500 to build and had seating for a congregation of 500. The Salvation Army established a separate corps in Skegness, formed at a meeting in a High Street café in 1913.

A citadel was later opened in the High Street on 9th March 1929.

In 1839, a Penny School was opened on the west side of Roman Bank, where now there are the school cottages. The school building was enlarged in 1850, but was still considered *'a poking little hole'*. The Earl of Scarbrough donated a new site, on the corner of Ida Road and Roman Bank, for a larger Skegness National Endowed School. He also gave £500 to help with the building costs. The school, which opened in 1880, had room for about 200 pupils. Abraham Porter was the schoolmaster. In addition to this larger school, the County Council Infants' School was opened on Cavendish Road in 1908. Skegness also had some private boarding schools. Essendon Girls' School was at the north end of Rutland Terrace where the Masonic Hall is today. Brythwen High School was opened in 1899 in what, until recently, was the Lyndhurst Club on the corner of Lumley Avenue and Algitha Road. Several more private boarding schools opened their doors between the wars, the most notable being the Orient Girls' School and the Preparatory School for Boys on Scarbrough Avenue, occupying what is now the Charnwood Hotel and adjacent buildings; the Inglewood Preparatory School in Ida Road and the Seacroft Preparatory School for Boys on Seacroft Esplanade (now a nursing home).

Skegness was administered by the *'Skegness Parish Vestry'* until 1885, but then a Local Government Board was elected to take over the running of the town. This lasted for ten years until 1895 when Skegness became an Urban District Council. At a meeting of the *Parish Vestry* in 1882, twelve local men were appointed to serve as constables. All had other occupations. A Police Station was built on Roman Bank that same year, at a cost of £1,200. It had three cells and a courtroom for occasional use. There was also suitable accommodation for the Inspector, Mr. Eggleston. In 1908 Skegness was allocated its own petty sessional court that was convened only during the summer months. A new courthouse was built in 1929, next to the Police Station, which was used all the year round.

Only half of the Earl's 'Grand Plan' was developed. Scarbrough Avenue, which the Earl saw as the main shopping street and the central avenue in the original plan, became the edge of the new Skegness. The shopkeepers wanted the shops, originally planned for Scarbrough Avenue, to be nearer to the railway station. They wanted the excursionists to pass them on the way to the beach, so the private houses that had been built on Lumley Road were gradually turned into shops. However, with the exception of the Market Place, the Winter Gardens and the Aquarium, the layout of the town was almost perfectly in accordance with his plan, even to the position of the ground plan for the reading room and the school. The Market Place came to nothing because it was realised that the Skegness hinterland was too limited and was already served by markets at Wainfleet, Alford and Burgh, although the market in Burgh was much in decline. A fortnightly Cattle Market was opened near the railway station, but that only lasted a few years. George Ball, an auctioneer, started a new cattle market near the Gasworks in 1923, but by 1937 that too had closed.

In 1870, the first Post Office in Skegness was opened in the High Street, run by Mrs Almond. In 1888, the Post Office was moved to Lumley Road and then in 1905 it was rehoused on the corner of Algitha Road and Roman Bank. A new General Post Office and Telephone Exchange was built on the opposite side of Roman Bank in 1929. As well as the Post Office, Kelly's 1885 directory also listed 'Sutton and Co. Parcels Delivery' with Thomas Locke as the agent.

Bill Berry opened a cycle shop on the High Street in 1895. It later became High Street Motor Engineers. By 1910, a charabanc had already replaced the horse drawn bus service from the Lion Hotel to the Royal Oak at Winthorpe. In 1922, Bill Berry started the town bus service. He sold the bus company to Tom Cary in 1925.

Skegness Steam Laundry Co. was established on Roman Bank in 1877. It was progressively enlarged to become eventually Fenlands Laundries. The Hygienic Sanitary Laundry Co. opened in Wainfleet Road. Mr J. Hunter was the managing director in 1907, but unlike its rival it survived only until the 1930s.

The first edition of the *Skegness Herald* appeared in 1882. Until then the main source for news and advertising was the *Stamford Mercury*. The office for the *Skegness Herald* was situated at the back of 17 Lumley Road where John Avery printed and published the paper that appeared on Fridays. It was the only local paper for more than twenty years until in 1909 Charles Henry Major published the *Skegness News*. A few years later in 1915 Major took over the *Skegness Herald* but it only lasted another couple of years before it ceased publication in 1917. The Boston based *Lincolnshire Standard* launched the *Skegness Standard* in 1922.

Not everything in the new town was purely functional. There was an ornate fountain complete with gaslights standing in Lumley Square. It was moved to the newly completed Marine Gardens (now the site of the Embassy Theatre) in 1888 and later, minus the gaslights, it became the main water feature in the Fairy Dell Paddling Pool. The planners of the new town decided that Lumley Road (which had become the main shopping street) needed a focal point where it met the Grand Parade. It was decided that a Clock Tower would be built to commemorate Queen Victoria's Diamond Jubilee. The clock tower was designed by the Liverpool architect Edmund White and built by W.H. Parker & Son of Boston in 1899. It rises to a height of 56 feet and the design makes reference in the upper part to Big Ben at the House of Commons in London. The mixture of brick and stone in the lower part was a reminder of all the new buildings that were being built at the time of its erection. The Countess of Scarbrough unveiled the completed tower on 11th August 1899.

Chapter Six

Catering for the influx of visitors to Skegness

When the trains first began bringing large numbers of excursionists to Skegness, there was nothing for the visitors to do, except breathe in the invigorating air, walk along the beach or paddle in the sea. Those not staying in the hotels found that there were no catering facilities for the increasing number of day-trippers arriving during the summer. The resident population of Skegness was still only just over 350 in 1883, but it was not long before enterprising locals began to set up stalls offering refreshments and other commodities, a practice the Earl of Scarbrough tried to stop when he started building his new town.

Not everyone regarded the changes in Skegness as positive. Some looked upon the influx of visitors with *'a feeling somewhat akin to dread'*. The local newspaper reported that *'the excursionists drop down upon the place in numbers so overwhelming as to leave the town as bare of nutriment as was Egypt after a visitation of locusts'*. It also claimed that the change in character of Skegness was *'driving away respectable families who were wont to visit the quiet spot'*. By 1883, the disquiet had not abated. The *Skegness Herald* deplored the arrival of *'shoals of labourers on the Sabbath'*.

Before the introduction of the Earl of Scarbrough's 'Grand Plan' there were already Bathing Machines installed both at the Vine and the New Hotel. By the beginning of the nineteenth century the Vine had a garden and a bowling green. However, all the activities were designed to entertain the wealthy classes. The village of Skegness could still only boast of having three shopkeepers. It had hardly changed from the small agricultural village it had been for many decades.

It was obvious to the Earl and his agent, Tippet, that there was a need to provide amenities that would attract the visitors to his new resort. In the original plan for the new town, provision was made for

97

the construction of a pier. This was commissioned in 1879 and completed in 1881. The Pier was a magnificent 1842 feet in length and had plenty of comfortable shelters and seating along the full length on both sides. At the furthest point there was a very handsome Pavilion, refreshment rooms, a bookstall and shops where presents might be purchased. The concert room in the Pavilion had seating for up to 600 people. Here concerts were given daily including on Sundays. There was a special staircase that led from the pier deck to the level of the roof of the concert hall, where the visitors could enjoy a panoramic view of the new town in one direction and gaze out over the German Ocean in the other.

A year after the opening of the Pier, the Skegness Steamboat Company was formed. It chartered a number of paddle steamers running trips to Grimsby, Boston and King's Lynn. A landing stage was built at the end of the Pier and visitors could embark and land three hours either side of high tide. In 1883 the 'May', one of the largest paddle steamers on the east coast operated throughout the summer, providing luxury accommodation for up to 255 passengers. There were day trips to Hunstanton for 3s (15p) and to the Lynn Well lightship, including a landing and a look around the ship for 1/6d (7.5p). The day trips to Hunstanton sometimes allowed time for a visit to Royal Sandringham. The 'Spindrift' was another popular vessel using the pier head, but the last of the paddle steamers was probably the favourite, the 'Privateer' of Boston. However, during the latter part of the nineteenth century sandbanks had been building up in the Wash, making wide detours necessary. In addition, the pier landing stage became unsafe. When in 1911 the landing stage was dismantled, the company could not afford to replace it. The 'Privateer' operated from the beach for one more summer, but then the service was discontinued.

The Skegness Turkish Hot and Cold Swimming Baths were opened in Scarbrough Avenue in 1883 at the cost of £4,000. There were separate pools for ladies and gentlemen, private baths and the Turkish Baths. The water supply was through a gravity pipeline from the sea, boosted by a suction pump. When mixed bathing became permissible at the beginning of the twentieth century, the ladies' pool was boarded over to become the King's Theatre and the men's pool was opened to both sexes. There was a reading room, open Monday to Friday from 9 am to 6 pm, situated in Scarbrough Avenue, adjacent to the Skegness Baths where the holidaymakers could, for the charge of one penny, read the daily and weekly newspapers and various periodicals.

On the site of an old coal yard, just west of the Grand Parade, the new Pleasure Gardens, with a lake and various paths through the lawns and flowerbeds, was laid out towards the end of the 1870s. At one end was a Pavilion containing dining rooms, a concert hall and a ballroom. In front of the Pavilion was a bandstand where orchestras and brass bands occasionally played. The gardens were a green oasis where the holidaymakers could relax away from the hustle and bustle of the sea front. In 1888, south of the pier, the Earl of Scarbrough arranged for grass and shrubs to be planted. His idea was to give the Parade a more pleasing aspect, but more importantly, it was hoped that the build-up of sand that had occurred since the retaining wall was built a year earlier would be halted. This area became known as the Marine Gardens.

Each year, from around the 1890s, the Battle of the Flowers was held. This was carnival time and Lumley Road and the Parades were garlanded with flags and flowers. Many people came to see the passing procession. A switchback railway was built on a large part of the Jungle frontage on North Parade in 1885, but was dismantled in 1912. There was a fairground on the central beach where, in 1910, Cartwright's Great Wheel was among the attractions. On the North Parade in the 1920s Charlie Brewster's Ducking Pond caused much merriment among the spectators. When a wooden ball hit the bull's-eye, the fall guy in a wet suit fell through the divided seat and ended up with a good soaking. Jim Lewis' Mini Zoo was another attraction on North Parade in the early 1920s, with a bear, baboon, monkeys, parrots and other 'wonders' of the jungle.

It was in 1900 that Fred Clements brought his first concert party to Skegness. Within a few years, he had become the resort's leading entertainments entrepreneur. His first 'theatre' was the Happy Valley on the sands. He then leased the Lawn Theatre, built in 1911 by Bass, the owners of the Hildred's Hotel. He also built the Arcadia Theatre in 1911 and the Tower Theatre in 1921. Clements believed that motion pictures could well have a profitable future and the Tower was used as a cinema almost from the start. After the Tower Theatre was built, the Lawn Theatre was let to Henri DeMond, who turned it into a picture theatre. The Lawn Theatre continued until 1934, when it was closed and the building incorporated into the Hildred's Hotel. John Henry Canning, a Skegness builder and developer, opened the Central Hall on Roman Bank in 1911. This was used for public meetings, concerts and dances. In the 1920s, Miss Nora Canning held dancing classes there. Later it was converted into the Central Cinema. Burrows and Chilvers' Chalet Theatre stood on the edge of the Jungle on North Parade in the early 1920s and, for several summers, this was the venue for high-class musical concerts. Before the building of the Chalet, they had an open-air pitch in Marine Gardens, Grand Parade, where candles in ornamental bowls strung between poles illuminated evening performances.

H.B. Sykes of Derby founded the Derbyshire Poor Children's Seaside Home in the 1890s. The first summer he brought parties of children from poor homes in Derby for a week's holiday in rented accommodation in the High Street, but later built a much larger establishment on Scarbrough Avenue. The curative qualities of the bracing breezes were *in high repute among the medical men of London and the Midlands for its good effect in cases of chest complaints and rheumatism'.* The Nottingham and Notts convalescent home for men was built in 1891, followed by one for children eighteen months later with funds provided by Sir C. Seely. Then there was Lady Scarbrough's Home for Women and Children at Seaview, where patients paid only 5/- (25p) a week. The Holiday Home for Nottingham Girls was opened on Brunswick Drive in 1912. The National Deposit Friendly Society's Convalescent Home was built on North Parade in 1927 and, one year later, the Derbyshire

Miners' & Friendly Societies' Convalescent Home was opened, all offering a chance to recuperate at the seaside. In 1929, the Nottingham Poor Children's' Holiday Home moved to new premises on Roseberry Avenue after several years in tents and huts. The 1920s was also the decade when tents and caravans came into fashion thus providing more accommodation and freedom for the visitors to come and go as they pleased.

For those who wanted to record their trip to the seaside, there were photographic booths. The earliest known professional photographer in Skegness was Charles Smyth who was established in the High Street in 1882. He later moved into premises on the new Lumley Road. During the season he also had a seafront studio in a wooden hut on the south side of the Clock Tower. Samuel Charles Burnham had another wooden studio on the north side of the Pier from about 1890 until his death in 1913. However, probably the best-known photographic business was that of Alfred Wrate who set up his business at 17 Lumley Road in 1907. Later, the business was run by his wife and family and was the most successful photography firm in Skegness for more than half of the twentieth century. Walking snapshots became popular at the seaside just after the First World War and Mrs Amelia Wrate was soon leading the field. Young men and women in bright orange striped blazers caught the trippers on the parades and esplanades snapping as many as 100 a day. The prints were ready two hours later.

Augustine and Frank Fravigar, of Italian descent, came from Boston to sell ice cream on the beach in 1880. They paid 2/6d (12.5p) a year for their pitch. Three generations of the family sold ice cream, which for many years they manufactured in Alexandra Road. Before cornets and wafers were invented, the ice cream was dispensed in what looked like thick glass eggcups.

The Cricket Ground, near to the railway station was acquired in 1879. In 1886, the Australian Touring Eleven cricket team played on this ground. Sixteen excursion trains brought hundreds of spectators to Skegness. The first game of golf was played on the Seacroft Golf Course in 1898. This was a nine-hole course that was later extended to 18 holes. At the other end of the town, the North Shore Golf Course was completed in 1910. The watching of horse racing on the sands was still a popular pastime, with races taking place on the sands outside the Sea View Hotel. Early in 1899 Bill Berry was part of a syndicate of local businessmen who brought the first car to Skegness. The journey from London with the car travelling at 12 mph took three and a half days. The Daimler was used to provide short rides for visitors. Later, in 1905, motorcar racing took place on the hard sands of Skegness beach. The first meeting was organised by the Notts. Automobile Club. The cars raced along a straight mile long track, with wire netting over the soft sandy patches. In 1929, the course was changed to a two kilometre oval track with hairpin bends at each end and transferred to the north end of the beach.

As the town continued to grow, so did the selection of restaurants and coffee rooms to provide the visitors with refreshments. The Casino, on North Parade, was one such restaurant. It was established in 1922 on the site of an earlier dance hall known as the 'Alhambra' that had been built in 1911. As well as a ballroom, the Casino specialized in party catering with seating for 920 at a single sitting. As the years continued, more ideas to appeal to the visitors and residents were to be put in place. In December 1921 the Skegness Council Surveyor, R.H. Jenkins, presented his master scheme for the development of the foreshore that had been purchased from the Earl of Scarbrough for the modest sum of £15,750. Between 1923 and 1937 there were fifteen years of development on what was basically just sand dunes. These sand dunes were transformed into a boating lake, a bathing pool, esplanades, lawns, a rose garden, a ballroom and restaurants, walks and waterways, car parks and bowling greens. This was the biggest transformation to take place in Skegness since the Earl of Scarbrough's original 'Grand Plan.' However, that, together with the developments undertaken by the young entrepreneur, Billy Butlin, who arrived in Skegness in 1925, is another story.

Chapter Seven

Why did it happen?

The small, obscure, agricultural village of Skegness became a flourishing seaside town by the end of the nineteenth century. Would this have happened anyway over a period of time or were there factors that turned Skegness into the main seaside town rather than Ingoldmells or Chapel St Leonard's?

The decline in agriculture in the early nineteenth century coinciding with the rise in the cult of sea bathing made it only a matter of time before some villages close to the Lincolnshire coast became seaside resorts. The first Lincolnshire village to offer facilities for people wanting to visit the sea was Freiston Shore. It became popular because of its position close to Boston. In a county where the roads were not good, the upper classes could travel to the port of Boston and then without too much difficulty on to Freiston Shore, two or three miles away. It was already popular in the 1780s and remained so for over a century, but the gradual silting up of that part of the coast and improved access to other places along the coast meant that its popularity was dwindling by the middle of the nineteenth century.

The first hotel in Skegness was built in 1770. It was about three quarters of a mile from the little village and certainly not on the road to anywhere in particular, so one can only assume that it was built to attract visitors to the coast. As with the visitors to Freiston Shore, they would have been from the upper classes as it would have been well nigh impossible for any of the working classes, at the end of the eighteenth century, to have the means to travel to the coast unless they were within walking distance. By 1805, a second hotel, built at the eastern end of the main village street, was ready to receive visitors. So we see that even at the beginning of the nineteenth century the village of Skegness was undergoing a gradual change. That change remained gradual for at least another fifty years.

So why did Skegness, rather than other coastal villages in the area become the major seaside resort? One important fact was that one man, the Earl of Scarbrough, owned a large acreage of land close to the village. He could use the land as he wished. Until the middle of the nineteenth century, he and his ancestors had been quite happy to use the land for agriculture. However, with the decline in agriculture, he needed to find another way to safeguard his wealth. The 9th Earl was a man of vision and he could see the potential in moving away from agriculture and towards tourism and the sea. He, along with his agent Tippet, drew up a 'Grand Plan' for the area running north from the village High Street to approximately where Castleton Boulevard is today, bounded on the west by Roman Bank and on the east by the sea. He wanted to make sure that the new town had a real structure and that the village would not just grow haphazardly.

Although he had the vision, he could not build the new town without builders, craftsmen and labourers. There were some, in Skegness, who could act as labourers, but the craftsmen would have to come from outside the village. Some could have been found in the local small towns, such as Boston, Louth or Alford, but others would have to come from further afield. From the middle of the nineteenth century, there was a railway station at Burgh le Marsh and, by 1871, there was a station at Wainfleet. This allowed some craftsmen from the industrial Midlands to travel to within six or seven miles of the Lincolnshire coast, but the rest of the journey would have had to be completed on foot or they might have been able to take advantage of the transport sent by the hotels to meet the trains.

It was important that the railway should come to Skegness. The Earl had envisaged visitors coming to his new town in huge numbers. A station in Skegness would allow them easy access to the sea and the town. The Earl would not have had a good return for his initial high investment, if there were not the visitors to take advantage of the growing number of amenities that would be on offer. If the railway to the coast were to have gone to Mablethorpe and bypassed Skegness, then it is possible that the Earl's 'Grand Plan' would, at best, have taken many extra years to come to fruition and at worst, it would have been scrapped altogether. Tippet obviously worked hard at lobbying the Railway Company because on 28th July 1873 the new rail extension from Wainfleet to Skegness was opened.

Now that the railway had arrived the Earl could increase the advertising of his new town by placing maps and other advertising material in the railway stations of the East Midlands, Lincolnshire and Yorkshire and even at King's Cross. This would bring his 'Grand Plan' to the attention of a much wider range of people, not only artisans and businessmen, but also the much needed visitors that the Earl wanted in his new town. All came in huge numbers. A great many settled in the town, so that eight years after the arrival of the railway, the population had quadrupled. In 1871 (two years before the arrival of the railway to Skegness) 59% of the 349 inhabitants of the village were either born there or came from within a five-mile radius. By the time of the 1881 census, there were approximately 1,000 people living in Skegness who were born outside that five-mile radius.

The slow gradual change that had taken place over the previous one hundred years was suddenly catapulted into ten years of upheaval. The speed with which the building boom took place was unprecedented along this part of the coast. After 10 years half of the Earl's 'Grand Plan' had become a reality. There were the houses; new hotels and lodging houses; restaurants and coffee shops; wide streets; attractive Parades and Pleasure Gardens; a Pier and several amenities for the visitors.

However, why was only half of the Earl's plan completed? It has been difficult to find any information giving a positive reason for this. It was obvious from the plan that the Earl saw Scarbrough Avenue as the central avenue. It is the widest of all the streets and has the church at its central point. Yet the streets to the north of Scarbrough Avenue were never completed. We can only guess at a reason. It is probable that the depression, which affected the whole of England, had a knock on effect for the new town. The frantic building schedule came practically to a halt in 1884 when only ten houses were built that year. The depression continued for many years. As we have seen in Chapter Four, the builder T.S. Kassel was declared bankrupt after being unable to sell most of Rutland Terrace. If, as has been suggested, other builders faced similar problems, they would not have been available to continue building even if the Earl had wanted to. There was also a decline in the number of visitors coming to the town. This obviously had an effect on local businesses, but would it have had an effect on the overall building plan? We know that the Earl envisaged Scarbrough Avenue as his main shopping street, but the shopkeepers wanted their shops to be closer to the station so that the excursionists would pass by on their way to the sea. Most of the shops were opened along Lumley Road and the High Street, thus moving the centre of the town away from Scarbrough Avenue. The symmetry had gone out of the original plan; therefore, it was perhaps not seen as essential to continue. Moreover, in 1884, the 9th Earl died, but Tippet was still there and the 10th Earl was keen, so it seems unlikely that was the reason. It was not until the 1920s and 1930s that attention was turned again to the development of the area north of Scarbrough Avenue. By that time the town planners seemed to have other ideas for the layout of that part of Skegness so the Earl's Grand Plan was never completed.

We have seen that with the rise in the new cult of sea bathing it would only have been a matter of time before one or more of the coastal villages would have turned into a seaside town. However, there were three main factors, in the middle of the nineteenth century, which helped to turn the village of Skegness into the leading resort on the southeastern part of the Lincolnshire coast. The first was that the coastline was gradually changing causing the area around Freiston Shore to silt up. There was a decline in the number of visitors to that area, but since people were now interested in being by the sea, there was a need to find other parts of the coastline with the potential to become a seaside resort. The second was the fact that the Earls of Scarbrough owned a substantial amount of land to the north of the village. The 9th Earl saw that a change of land use from the traditional grazing to a well-planned new town with an emphasis on tourism would, in the longer term, safeguard his wealth. He was not afraid to back his plan with a large amount of money, knowing that the initial outlay would reap huge rewards. However, even this would not have guaranteed a thriving town if the Earl and Tippet had not persuaded the Railway Company to bring the railway directly to Skegness. It was the railway that allowed for the holidaymakers and day-trippers to come to the new town. Without them, the small obscure agricultural village of Skegness would not have been transformed into the thriving coastal town that it had become by the end of the nineteenth century.

Bibliography

Avery, John. *Avery's Popular Penny Guide to Skegness, with map, directory &c.* 2nd ed. Skegness, J. Avery, 1894.

Dutton, George H.J. *Ancient and Modern Skegness and District. A topographical, historical and entertaining accout etc.* Skegness: Dutton, 1922.

Gurnham, Richard. *The Creation of Skegness as a Seaside Resort,* Lincolnshire History & Archaeology, Vol.7. Sleaford: Society of Lincolnshire History and Archaeology, 1972.

Hewson, Julie E. *Who were the Skegness pioneers? A Study of people who settled in the New Town of Skegness 1871–1881,* Lincolnshire History & Archaeology, Vol. 21. Sleaford: Society of Lincolnshire History and Archaeology, 1986.

Kelly, W. *Kelly's Post Office Directory of Lincolnshire.* London: W. Kelly, 1849.

Kelly, W. *Kelly's Directory of Lincolnshire.* London: W. Kelly, 1885.

Kime, Winston. *The Book of Skegness: Ingoldmells, Addlethorpe and Chapel St. Leonards.* Buckingham: Barracuda, 1986.

Kime, Winston. *Skeggy! The Story of an East Coast Town.* Skegness: Seashell Books, 1969.

Kime, Winston. *Skegness in old Photographs – collected by Winston Kime.* Stroud: Sutton, 1992.

Kime, Winston. *The Lincolnshire Seaside.* Stroud: Sutton Publishing Ltd, 2005.

Kime, Winston. *The Skegness Date Book 1850–2000 compiled by Winston Kime.* Skegness: Skegness Town Council, 2006.

Lincolnshire County Council. *A Place with a Past – Church Farm Museum.* Lincoln: Lincolnshire County Council, c. 2005.

Ludlam, A.J. *Railways to Skegness: The East Lincolnshire Railway.* Usk: Oakwood Press, 1991.

Robinson, David. *The Book of the Lincolnshire seaside: The Story of the Coastline from the Humber to the Wash.* Buckingham: Baron, 2001.

Thirsk, Joan. *English Peasant Farming: The Agrarian History of Lincolnshire from Tudor to recent times.* London: Routledge & Kegan Paul, 1957.

White, William. *History, Gazetteer, and Directory of Lincolnshire.* Sheffield: printed for the author, 1826.

White, William. *History, Gazetteer, and Directory of Lincolnshire.* Sheffield: printed for the author, sold by W. White, 1856.

White, William. *New Map of Lincolnshire, Published with his History, Gazetteer, and Directory of the County of Lincolnshire.* Sheffield and London: W. White, 1872.

White, William. *History, Gazetteer, and Directory of the County of Lincolnshire, including the city and diocese of Lincoln and separate descriptions of all the boroughs, towns etc.* Sheffield: W. White, 1882.

Miscellaneous

Dutton, George H.J. *Scrapbooks* (unpublished copies on display in Church Farm Museum, accessed 2004).

Neller, Ruth. *Skegness Chronology 1526–1991* (Skegness Library).

U3A. *Notes on the Local History of Skegness – From the earliest times to 1939* (Booklet produced by Skegness U3A Local History Group, 2005).

National Railway Museum, Quote by the Duke of Wellington in 1829. York

Around Lincolnshire – Skegness. Internet site (Accessed 2005).

Historical Skegness. Internet Site (Accessed 2005).

Skegness Town Council   *History of Skegness* (History of Skegness by Winston Kime) http://www.visitoruk.com/skegness/timeline.html (Accessed 2005).

MEN OF INFLUENCE

The Earls of Scarbrough

Mr. Henry Vivian Tippet

Mr. Rowland Henry Jenkins

The Earls of Scarbrough
By Carrol Morris, Kenneth Wilkinson and James Mackley

The early years

The interest of the Earl of Scarbrough's ancestors in Skegness goes back a long way. Winston Kime refers to Nicholas Saunderson (later Viscount Castleton) as owning land in Skegness in the time of Elizabeth I (1558–1603).[185] In 1631 Nicholas Saunderson, Viscount Castleton, owned half the land in Skegness. The Scarborough Earldom was created in 1681 in favour of Richard, Viscount Lumley, who commanded the forces of James II at the Battle of Sedgmoor, the last large battle fought on English soil. He was also one of the seven men (the Immortal Seven) who signed the invitation to William of Orange to secure the liberties of England, by intervention against the Government of James II in 1688.[186]

In 1690, Skegness came into the possession of the Saunderson family who had settled north of Lincoln at Saxby-by-Spital.

In 1723 James Saunderson of Saxby who had become Earl of Castleton died without heir, leaving his great estates to his cousin, Thomas Lumley the 3rd Earl of Scarborough. The land around Skegness was prosperous and in 1739, it provided 17% of the Earl's total income.

According to a plaque in St. Clement's Church, Viscount Castleton was patron of the Skegness living at the time of the arrival of Thomas Thompson as rector in 1667. The patronage passed to Thomas Lumley-Saunderson, who became the third Earl of Scarbrough, in 1739. The living remained under the patronage of the Earls of Scarbrough until the death of the 12th Earl in 2004.

---

[185] Winston Kime, *The Book of Skegness*.
[186] T. W. Beastall, *A North Country Estate: The Lumleys and Saundersons as Landowners, 1600–1900*, p. 1.

The 9th and 10th Earls: 1856 to 1945

Richard George became the 9th Earl of Scarborough on 25 October 1856; he had married Frederica the younger daughter of Andrew Drummond during October 1846. It was during the latter part of the 9th Earl's life that he conceived the idea of developing Skegness.

In the 1870s, the 9th Earl had a Grand Plan (*see* Map 4) for Skegness. The first stage of this plan involved the building of new houses between Roman Bank and the sea. As development spread, tenant farmers were forced to leave the land. Church Farm suffered lightly and the first effects of the development were when the Earl had to sell a small part of a field to make way for the railway in 1873.

The work was continued by the 10th Earl, who succeeded his father in 1884. Although the major part of the Grand Plan had been set into motion, the Marine Gardens were opened in 1888 and the Clock Tower was built to mark the Queen's Diamond Jubilee in 1897 (completed in 1899).

After the First World War, with peace and change, the Earl decided the time had come for him to get back to his main interests: agriculture and land ownership. The seaside was no longer to be part of his activities, so he offered to sell the whole of the foreshore to Skegness Urban District Council at a bargain price of £15,100. This was referred to at the time as "The Sale of the Century".

School and Street names

Until recently, the largest secondary school in Skegness was called the "Earl of Scarbrough School" (now St. Clement's).

Many of the roads in Skegness are named after the Earl of Scarbrough's family. **Scarbrough** Avenue was designed to be the main street in Skegness under the 9th Earl's Grand Plan. The shopkeepers had other ideas and set up in **Lumley** Road, which was on the main route from the station to the beach. As has already been mentioned, Lumley was the family name of the first Earl of Scarbrough. In addition to Lumley Road, the family gave its name to Lumley Avenue,

Lumley Crescent and Lumley Square (and also the Lumley Hotel).

The 9th Earl was the son of Charlotte Mary **Beresford**, who gave her name to Beresford Avenue, Close and Crescent. He married **Frederica**, youngest daughter of Andrew **Drummond**, grandson of the Duke of Rutland, and both father and daughter are commemorated by roads in Seacroft. His four daughters were named **Algitha**, **Ida**, **Lilian** and **Sibell** Lumley. Algitha Road and Ida Road were built in the 1880s. Lilian Road and Sibell Road were the names given on the Grand Plan to the two roads to the north and parallel to Scarbrough Avenue, which were never built.

The 10th Earl married Cecilia whose father was **Cecil** Gardiner. Cecil Avenue was named after them. Their daughter, **Serena** Mary **Barbara**, born 1901, gives her names to two short roads leading from South Parade to Drummond Road. She was the first daughter born to a reigning Earl for 150 years.

Castleton (first Viscount Castleton and then Earl of Castleton) was the titular name of the Saunderson family, the ancestors of the Earls of Scarbrough, who owned the land in Skegness. Nicholas, son of George, Viscount Castleton, the first of the family to be the patron of the Skegness living, married Elizabeth Wray of **Glentworth,** after which Glentworth Crescent is named.

The family seat is **Sandbeck** House near Rotherham. **Firbeck** is the nearest village to it. Sandbeck and Firbeck Avenue are the names of avenues in the south of the town.[187]

---

[187] Though not relevant to the Earls of Scarbrough, our research has uncovered the following information about the origins of other street names in Skegness: the streets in what was known as Kirk's Estate, between Sea View and North Shore Roads, are all named after famous golf courses, i.e. St. Andrews, Sunningdale, Hoylake, Brancaster and Muirfield. It will be observed, too, that they are not roads or avenues, but "drives", which are also associated with the game.

Prince George Street got its name in rather an unusual way. It was known as Lumley Back Road before the First World War, but the late C.H. Major, who had a printing works there, did not like "Back Road" on his notepaper. He asked the Council to give it a new name and when they refused, he christened it Prince George Street. Other tradesmen followed his example so it became generally known as Prince George Street. The Council finally bowed to the inevitable and put up a new street plate.

Mr Henry Vivian Tippet and his contribution to the development of Skegness
By Kenneth Wilkinson

The man chiefly responsible for the development of Skegness as a resort town in the late nineteenth century was the estate agent of the 9th Earl of Scarbrough, Mr H.V. Tippet.

Richard George became the 9th Earl of Scarborough on 25 October 1856. It was during the latter part of the Earl's life that he conceived the idea of developing Skegness. It was his agent, Mr Henry Vivian Tippet, who, in 1876, assisted by Mr Gilbert J. Dashper, Clerk to the Local Board, had plans drawn up for changing the village of Skegness into a popular resort.

The development included Lumley Road, Algitha Road, Ida Road, Scarbrough Avenue, Lumley Avenue, Rutland Road, the Pleasure Gardens, Pier, Cricket Ground, the Seafront and Marine Gardens.

Mr Tippet arranged to let the lands on building leases of 99 years. Several shops in Lumley Road were let at a ground rent of

18/4d per annum and houses on the Grand Parade for 10/- per annum.

As early as June of 1876, smallholders were building on their land and on 4 December 1876, Mr Tippet wrote to his Lordship: "Everything now bids fair I think for Skegness to go forward".

As well as the road building, the water supply and sewage disposal were the responsibility of the Earl of Scarbrough and Mr Tippet.

It was important for the development of the town that the railway came to Skegness and Mr Tippet did his utmost to ensure that it did so. In an effort to boost the sale of building plots, copies of the Skegness Town Plans were appearing on the following railway stations: Boston, Lincoln, Nottingham, Derby, Leicester, Sheffield, Leeds, Bradford, Doncaster, Peterborough, Grantham, Retford, Grimsby, as well as King's Cross Station.

A new hotel was opened on Good Friday 1880 opposite the Railway Station. It was named the Lumley Hotel. Other hotels in the town at that time were the Sea View, the Vine, the Ship, the Lion and the Hildreds, previously known as the New Inn.

The Skegness Pier was opened to the public in 1881. Thanks again to Mr Tippet, a Skegness market scheme was established off Roman Bank between Ida Road and Algitha Road, but when shopkeepers set up stalls in front of their shops on the main street Mr Tippet disapproved, because he wanted to preserve the appearance of the town; he received many complaints for his strict ruling on this.

Mr Tippet had left his home in Yorkshire to live in Skegness and an estate office was set up in the town at a cost of £1,400. Later he sat on the Local Board.

In 1887, work began on a sea wall to protect the town. This stretched from north of Sea View Lane to Derby Avenue. Stone for the wall came mainly from a quarry near to the ruins of Roche Abbey and some from the Abbey itself. Both are near to the mining village of Maltby, South Yorkshire. Transportation was by Traction Engine.

Mr Tippet died in 1902 aged 68. His son, also Vivien, was for many years assistant town clerk of the town council.

Skegness Local Board 1887: Mr Tippet seated second from the right

Mr Rowland Henry Jenkins and his contribution to the development of the Skegness Foreshore
By Kenneth Wilkinson

Born in Kent, Mr Jenkins came to Skegness in 1912 as Engineer and Surveyor to the Skegness Urban District Council. He was commissioned as a Captain in the Royal Engineers during the war, but continued to hold his post until retirement in December 1952, when he moved to Lymington in Hampshire then later to High Wycombe.

After a referendum in which the town's rate-payers voted in 1919, the Skegness Urban District Council bought the following from the Earl of Scarborough in 1922: the Pleasure Gardens, (later known as the Tower Gardens), for £8,600; the Marine Gardens and Seashore for £3,500; also the Sands Pavilion situated on the south side of the Clock Tower Pullover for £3,000. The total figure including legal costs came to £15,750.

Mr Jenkins already had a development scheme prepared for the foreshore and had it approved by the town councillors, and during the next 15 years he transformed bare sands and dunes into one of the leading resorts on the east coast. The amenities included an open air Bathing Pool, Boating Lake, Waterway, Tennis Courts, Bowling Greens, the Suncastle with Solarium and many rose gardens. To open up the foreshore, the old sand pullover (a gap in the dunes where the fishing boats were pulled through) leading from the Clock Tower was replaced by a wide asphalt road and footway. This was christened "Jenkins Pier" by local humorists. The Tower Esplanade paved the way for new seaward development.

Mr Jenkins could not only see what had to be done to put the town on a holiday map, but also had the ability to put his plans into effect, quickly and efficiently. He inspired others with his enthusiasm and in the years that were to follow was often not only leading the Councillors along the path he had planned, but was frequently giving them a helpful push in the desired direction.

Not without some misgivings, the Council approved the draft plan. Some of the smaller jobs were put in hand at once, but it was a year or two later that they came to consider the first really big item in the scheme: the boating lake was to cost a fearful lot of money and the Council had never spent that amount before, or at least not on a luxury like a boating lake. At a meeting seven wanted to build a boating lake, seven wanted the idea to be dropped. The chairman was called upon to give his casting vote and it was obvious that he was much undecided. In the seconds of painful silence whilst the scheme hung in the balance, up popped the Surveyor; he said that whilst it was not his business to influence the Council either way, he did have to mention that he had already placed substantial orders for materials in connection with the construction of the boating lake. This made up the chairman's mind and he voted for the work to begin. Mr Jenkins opened up the site straightaway in case there was any change of heart. Work went ahead at great speed and the first section of the lake was opened in the late summer of 1924. The Boating Lake was a great success with first year takings six times the estimate.

The outdoor Bathing Pool opened along with the Piazza building, later known as the Embassy, on Whit Monday 1928.

Mr Jenkins also formed the 1st Skegness Company of the Boys' Brigade and, as Captain, organized annual trips abroad. He was also a member of the Baptist Church and President of the Skegness Rotary Club in 1945/46. He resided in South View Close, before moving later to a house on Drummond Road overlooking the Golf Course.

He died aged seventy-five in 1962.

MAPS

Map 1: Skegness 1793

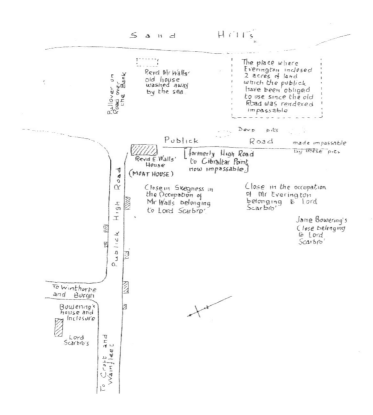

Skegness. 1793, based on a rough map referring to the Massingberd-Mundy lands

Map reproduced by kind permission of the late Winston Kime (sourced by William Kerr)

Map 2: Skegness 1849

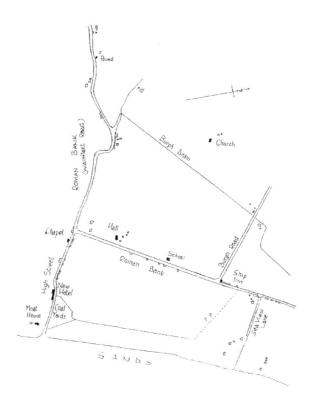

Skegness. Based on map of S. Hill and Son, Croft, 1849

Map reproduced by kind permission of the late Winston Kime (sourced by William Kerr)

Map 3: Area around Skegness 1849

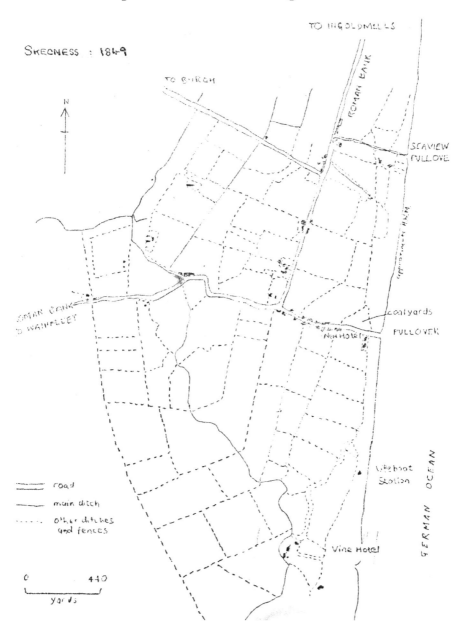

Map reproduced by kind permission of the late Winston Kime (sourced by William Kerr)

Map 4: The Earl of Scarbrough's Grand Plan 1878

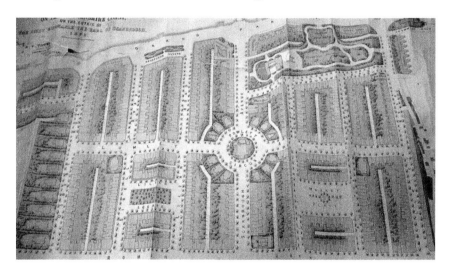

The map is the property of Lincolnshire County Council and is reproduced here with their kind
permission.

Map 5: Skegness 1906

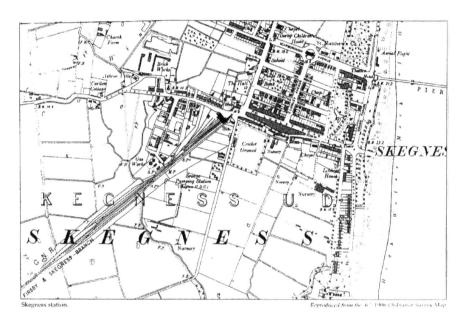

Map reproduced by kind permission of the late Winston Kime (sourced by William Kerr)

Printed in Great Britain
by Amazon

83775753R00081